Finding Your Prince
in a Sea of
Toads

Finding Your Prince in a Sea of Toads

How to Find a

Quality Guy Without

Getting Your

Heart Shredded

Dr. Kenneth Ryan

WinePressPublishing
Since 1991.

WinePress Publishing (PO Box 428, Enumclaw, WA 98022) functions only as book publisher. As such, the ultimate design, content, editorial accuracy, and views expressed or implied in this work are those of the author.

Disclaimer—I have not read all of each book that I recommend. Some materials have been recommended by others whom I respect, others may include just a concept that I have found helpful. Some materials I have read thoroughly. Everything you read must be carefully considered for truth before you apply it to your life.

Sex Is Like Duct Tape is an analogy from J. Budziszewski.
Men Are Like Waffles, Women Are like Spaghetti is an analogy from Bill and Pam Farrel.
The Love Test and Red Zone concepts are from Mike Long.

ISBN 13: 978-1-60615-095-5
ISBN 10: 1-60615-095-2
Library of Congress Catalog Card Number: 2009909173

Princes and Frogs
by Superchick

Obviously this song is about frogs and the book is about toads, but
the message is the same. Besides, toad doesn't rhyme with dog.

All princes start as frogs
All gentlemen as dogs
Just wait till it's plain to see
What we're growing up to be
Cuz some frogs will still be frogs
Some dogs will still be dogs
But some boys can become men
Just don't kiss us till then

You hate men is what you say
And I understand how you feel that way
All girls dream of a fairy tale
But what you got's like a used car salesman
Trying to conceal what's wrong
Behind a smile and a song
And I'm not saying that boys are not like that
But I think you should know
That some of us will grow

You found him is what you say
And we all want you to feel that way
But the frog you've got seems cute enough to kiss
And maybe frogs seem like that's all there is
But just because you haven't found your prince yet
Doesn't mean you're still not a princess
And what if your prince comes riding in
While you're kissin' a frog
What's he gonna think then?
**So look into his eyes
Are you a princess or a fly?**

Contents

Introduction

—✺

"No decision you make in life will affect your future happiness or misery more than the choice of who you marry."
—Anonymous

I READ THIS quote years ago and have always remembered it because of its simplicity and accuracy. The older I get the more it seems true. Women shred their hearts with poor relationship decisions made out of ignorance or desperation. Just as important as it is to choose a spouse wisely is the need for a woman to choose to be happy in her singleness, even if she would prefer to be married or have a boyfriend. The stakes are high. Happiness is on the line.

This book is based on the assumption that the vast majority of people have a dream of getting married. Whether age fifteen or fifty, male or female, rich or poor, any ethnic background, I believe most people at their core want to find a soulmate. Almost every woman wants a best friend with whom she can share her life; someone who ignites her passions; someone to whom it is safe to reveal her vulnerabilities, and who will be a loving parent to her children. She wants someone to grow old with and provide a love that grows and deepens over the years. She wants to rock on the porch in her old age with someone who knows her better than she knows herself. She wants someone who will quench her sexual appetite on a regular basis; someone who makes her heart skip when he enters the room.

This is a magnificent dream. I believe it is the dream of most people. If it does not describe you—at least in part—this might not be the book for you. However, if this is a reasonable description of you, my hope and intention for this book is that it might help you realize your dream and spare you many of the relational bumps, pitfalls, nightmares, and divorces that seem to be even much more common than the dream itself.

The big problem is the irrational, illogical path most people travel in their attempt to follow this dream. Culturally accepted practices for dating and finding a spouse are often risky paths that may not lead into the dream sequence. I hope to point out that many of the typical dating traditions and current practices will predictably lead to broken relationships and misery.

Fortunately, there are also many positive actions and attitudes you can adopt that will greatly increase your odds of landing somewhere in the dream. As my three daughters move into adulthood, my hope is they will each find a man with whom they can live this dream. It is my love for them and my love of that dream that motivates me to write. I want them to have every possible piece of inside advice to help them understand the dynamics of a relationship. I want them to always have the upper hand, by knowing how men think and respond in relationships contrasted with their own feminine mindset and responses. Once someone is wrapped up in the passions and emotions of a relationship, thinking rationally will be much more difficult.

Therefore, I want to communicate to my daughters and you while you're still thinking rationally so I can perhaps save you from yourself. Love and sex are perhaps the most powerful influencers of human behavior. You had better know what you are doing when you face these powerful forces. You can either get burned or enjoy the emotional ride of a lifetime.

The path of your life depends on thousands of small decisions you make every day. Since you have decided to read this book, I hope to steer you down paths that lead to happiness and away from the paths to misery. Prepare for a fulfilled happy life, less stressful dating, and perhaps you will find that dream spouse.

"We get too soon oldt, and too late schmardt." I think this saying is where I got the idea for "Smart" Marriages®. The hope is to help our youth get schmardt without having to learn the hard way—through their own terrible marriage mistakes.

—Diane Sollee, *smartmarriages.com*

Section One

DAMSEL IN DISTRESS

Why You Need this Book

Chapter 1

Finding Your Prince in a Sea of Toads

IF YOU ARE a single woman or a young girl who would like to be married one day, you look out into the vastness of humanity and wonder if there really is a prince in your future. On the surface, many of the guys around you seem to be reasonably attractive and normal. How could a person possibly sort through all of that maleness and stumble upon Mr. Right? It might seem overwhelming, and if you have been at it for awhile, you may already be discouraged. The stakes are high. Relationship decisions you make now can affect the future decision of who you marry. Are you on the road to happiness or misery?

Is this your dream?

If you have a very strong desire to find a wonderful husband with whom you will raise a family and have a lifetime of friendship, companionship, sexual passion, and adventure, this book is for you. It is for teenage girls, young women, and even older women. The principles apply to any single female. Note that sometimes I will refer to girls and boys, sometimes women and men. The terms are usually interchangeable so don't think I am not talking to you if I refer to a girl and you are a woman.

If you happen to be hoping for a great spouse, I think you will find this book to have a unique perspective on the process of finding one.

Since you picked up this book, you obviously have not yet successfully landed that mate.

If you are still young and years away from marriage, the principles in these pages will help you start to build confidence in your ability to interact with guys and establish healthy patterns for life.

Many women are careening wildly toward relationship disasters as they look for the husband of a lifetime. If most of your love life advice has come from *Cosmo*, *Entertainment Weekly*, movies, TV, and the street, I am certain that you will find my ideas to be radical and/or ridiculous.

Keep in mind, however, that you have not yet succeeded in your quest for marital bliss. Perhaps you are not even thinking of marital bliss but are ready to settle for any kind of relational satisfaction. If you have come up empty or injured by your efforts so far, maybe it is time for a new and rational approach. What do you have to lose? This might be one of the most important books you ever read. If nothing else, it will give you some intriguing conversation topics as you reevaluate your dating strategy. It will help you better understand what you are doing and where you are likely to end up.

If one of your dreams is to be happily married for a lifetime, this book offers you a rational plan to move you in that direction. It will keep your body and soul safe while allowing you the thrill and excitement of exploring new relationship possibilities. When you have a good plan and a thorough understanding of male/female relationships, you will feel empowered and gain confidence. The book offers a simple, quite do-able plan, yet it is certainly not easy to do. I am assuming the relationship topic is toward the very top of your list of concerns in life. With that positioning, I hope you are willing to invest the effort to put a workable plan into action. It will take effort to read this entire book and determine if it makes sense. You will need to honestly evaluate your current views on the topic to determine if my arguments and analogies are compelling enough to change or influence your way of thinking. I believe that much of your future happiness hangs on your decisions in this area, so I implore you to carefully consider the concepts that you might initially dismiss. Remember, if I am not challenging you with new ideas or ways of thinking, there is no point in reading the book. The purpose is to help you be well informed as you make some of the most critical decisions in your life. I hope that this book will be a turning point in your life—the time when you finally feel like you have hope and optimism in attaining your dream of sharing life with a great husband. If you have already experienced pain in this area, I hope you will come to understand why some of your actions, which seem to be endorsed by all of society, predictably resulted in the pain and regret you are feeling.

People often go with the flow because they know no other path. I would like to show you a road that is "less traveled." The road of this book is more likely to take you where you really want to go than the road most people are taking.

The Road Not Taken
By Robert Frost

Two roads diverged in a yellow wood,
And sorry I could not travel both
And be one traveler, long I stood
And looked down one as far as I could
To where it bent in the undergrowth.

Then took the other, as just as fair,
And having perhaps the better claim,
Because it was grassy and wanted wear;
Though as for that the passing there
Had worn them really about the same.

And both that morning equally lay
In leaves no step had trodden black.
Oh, I kept the first for another day!
Yet knowing how way leads on to way,
I doubted if I should ever come back.

I shall be telling this with a sigh
Somewhere ages and ages hence:
Two roads diverged in a wood, and I—
I took the one less traveled by,
And that has made all the difference.

Instant poem explanation: This classic poem describes how a single decision to follow your own way instead of following the crowd can alter the entire course of your life.

A meaningless but funny quote from Yogi Berra about choosing the right path says, "When you come to a fork in the road, take it."

First, the Bad News

The world has always been populated with undesirable guys, but their numbers and faults seem to be growing. The pickin's can be slim. Plenty of immature, self-centered, porno-warped, directionless mama's boys or macho thugs exist in our world. The odds are good that most of them will get married. Your goal is to avoid being one of the unfortunate, naïve victims who marries one of them out of desperation, ignorance, or poor judgment. The reduced number of quality guys makes it that much more important to have a plan so you are spending your time with the small number of quality princely guys rather than wasting your time on poor prospects—the toads. Otherwise, you might be blindly and randomly bouncing from toad to toad.

The Good News

There are still lots of good men out there looking for a precious woman just like you. They share your same dream of finding the love of a lifetime and the object of the game is for you to find each other. You can do important things that can increase your chances of finding the love of your life. Even though much of love and attraction is mysterious and irrational, your social life does not need to be random and irrational. At the same time, the process can be less stressful, less dangerous, more fun, and more effective than the old, ineffective methods you've been using.

If you have a good plan, you can markedly improve your chance of finding an excellent husband *and* living happily ever after with him. Notice that the goal contains two parts and they both depend on what you do while you are single. A key to this plan is that it is designed to keep you safe and satisfied both in your singleness and married life. It is not enough to simply find the right man. You want to head into your marriage fully equipped to make it successful. You can minimize the damaging scars and emotional baggage that are often picked up while people are single and add unnecessary stress and challenges to a marriage. Marriage is hard enough without extra baggage from previous relationships. Many of the negative consequences are unexpected surprises that we never anticipated. They sneak up on us when it is too late—sometimes years later. I invite you to think through your dating/ courtship plan with me.

Even though much of love and attraction is mysterious and irrational, your social life does not need to be random and irrational.

Throughout this book, I will often refer to undesirable men as toads. This denigrating term is intended to be very specific. By my definition, these guys are not desirable specifically as spouse material. They might be fine as friends, coworkers, classmates, teammates, hair stylists, surgeons, etc; however, I hope to convince you that if you want to be happily married for the rest of your life, you had better learn how to practically, efficiently, and enjoyably sift through the toads as you search for your prince. You want to spend most of your energy sorting through princely possibilities. It is not necessary or desirable to kiss lots of toads. In fact, you might get some emotional warts if you do. I will discuss that later.

I Am a Male

I grew up in the public schools of Michigan outside of Detroit. I had my first experience hearing a chorus of toads in junior high school locker rooms. I ran track and tried a few other sports so I got some bonus locker room time. Something about boys, nakedness, and sports brings up lots of talk about girls and sexuality. I played tennis in high school before enrolling at Michigan State University to become a veterinarian, and lived in the dorms for three years where I personally saw many toads in action.

By the time they leave high school, many toads have perfected their game. I watched with fascination the various approaches they used toward dating. Dorm room doors are left open in college so neighbors know they are welcome to wander in and discuss life. These candid conversations revealed the true relational aspirations of a large percentage of the guys. Women would have been appalled, but at the time, I was more fascinated and incredulous than appalled. I was too insecure about my own dating ineptitude to make many critical or moral judgments about what I was hearing and seeing.

Toads in Action

The most revealing thing I discovered was the huge disconnect between the way toads talked when they were with women compared to what they said when the girls were not around. I saw the inner workings of many male minds. They would brag about the manipulation techniques they used to gain sexual action from a girl. The girl honestly thought she was in the middle of a real relationship and many guys had no relationship ideas in mind. These guys were very good at what they did. They had learned to completely disguise their toadishness. Since most of them ended up married, plenty of women obviously cannot discern a toad from a prince. Society is cranking out toads at a greater rate now than ever before. Remember, many of these toads are attractive, charming, popular men. They do not come with visible warts to identify their true nature.

A Toad Is Born

Without any special training or societal influence, virtually every boy biologically is born to produce testosterone, hit puberty, start thinking about girls, and then become obsessed with the female gender to some degree or another. Boys instinctively dream about what it would be like to be sexually intimate with a girl or ultimately to experience sexual intercourse. Males generally have a very strong sex drive and that is a very good thing; however, without controlling influences, many men would behave like a musk ox—breeding aggressively at any opportunity without any other thought or worry.

Fortunately for women, children, and society, controlling factors have tempered this powerful, animalistic male sexuality. Every boy starts out with essentially this same wiring. If a boy does not have moral, ethical, spiritual, or practical reasons to control his sexual behavior, he will end up with the musk ox/toad level of sensitivity toward females. Many of the toads are toads because they are only operating from the practical restraints they find at any moment, i.e. they do not always follow their natural impulses because they might get slapped, scorned, or arrested. They learn to alter their behavior only to obtain their goal—not for any reason of right or wrong. They say whatever the girl wants to hear and will do whatever it takes to get her to submit to him. Perhaps you are thinking, "Those guys are obvious losers. I would not go out with men like that." Surprisingly, these guys find plenty of women who will fall for their games.

Chapter 2

Princes and Toads

SPECIES DESCRIPTIONS

TO HELP CLARIFY what I am talking about when I refer to "princes" and "toads" here are my definitions.

No Man Is All Prince or All Toad

If a guy was all prince … well, he doesn't exist. If a guy was all toad, you would have no interest in him anyway. A guy can be good at displaying his princely qualities on the surface or for a limited time. He knows you are looking for a prince and he wants to be attractive to girls. Perhaps, he is kind and confident, a hunk, funny, smart, interesting, easy to talk to, or anything else attractive to you. Every guy has some excellent qualities. Every guy also has some toad qualities in his pockets and in his soul. The game plan for possibly realizing your dream of a great marriage is to look for the important princely qualities of the guy while you discover his toad qualities without causing significant pain and damage to yourself in the process. Once you get a truer picture of him, you can make a more informed decision about whether to proceed with him in the relationship. If you dig deeper and deeper into his character and still like what you see, you are on the right track.

Prince

A prince is a guy who has enough good qualities to outweigh his bad qualities so that he would make a reasonably good husband for someone. Princes can be any IQ, athletic status, rich, poor, talkative, quiet, extroverted, introverted, cute, homely, a geek, a Grecian god, bald, fat, skinny, funny, or serious.

Princes are the guys you want to be sorting through in your quest for a great husband. Their primary traits are integrity and a moral compass. They know right from wrong and usually choose to do the right thing. Your long wish list of traits for your Mr. Wonderful should be negotiable, but those two must be non-negotiable. For example, if you find that man of integrity who thinks you are beautiful and would lay down his life for you, putting your needs above his own, you might want to cross "dimples" off your list of requirements for your husband.

A prince understands that his mission is to protect his princess at all costs. He will sacrifice his life or do whatever it takes for the good of the girl. He is perceptive enough to know the consequences of sexual activities and that his woman is at great risk emotionally and physically if she is sexually active with a man who doesn't have a lifetime commitment to her. Lastly, he has started to figure out that he himself is a threat to the girl. This sounds strange, but a prince is aware of the battle inside himself between his strong desire to be physically intimate and his conviction of what is right and best for the woman and her future marriage—maybe to him. He is willing to sacrifice his strong physical desires for the greater good of the woman. Even the most honorable guy will have this internal struggle between his natural urges and his need for restraint. In fact, if he does not have a simmering physical passion for you, I doubt that you would want to remain with him. The key is what he's willing to sacrifice for you and your potential long-term relationship. Relationships take planning and forethought from both of you and neither is easy. Integrity is what manhood is about; I hope that is the kind of husband you want.

Many of these princely types may not be a good match for you, but they would be a good match for somebody. You can enjoy spending time with men in this crowd, but you have to know how to find them because princes and toads are mixed together in life. The differences are often not obvious at first because many interactions with both types are superficial. Men can fake princely qualities easily for a short time.

Toad

A toad is a guy with a significant flaw or group of flaws that would make him a poor choice as a boyfriend or husband for almost anyone. I use toads instead of frogs because frogs are too cute for this metaphor. With their ugly warts, toads can be a little scary. Before you pick up a toad, you pause to wonder if you could possibly get warts yourself from handling them. Real amphibian toads don't transmit warts but people toads do.

Most toads will probably get married, as they will be charming enough to convince a woman to marry them; however, the wife will end up carrying the load. She might endure a poor marriage or end up with divorce. The best of this group might give his wife a mediocre marriage, but he does not begin to fulfill the dreams she has for raising a family and being loved unconditionally by a sensitive husband. He starts out okay but then pornography leaves him wondering why his wife doesn't look like the porn he watches, or he is more interested in watching sports than family activities, and he lets her handle the children and much of the work. He insisted on sexual activity while they were dating and she thought his lack of self-control was cute and exciting then; but now, he can't be trusted on business trips. It can get worse.

Some toads can be spotted from a mile away. You don't need a book to help avoid them. Unfortunately, many are very attractive on the outside. The warts are hidden under the surface. Many celebrities would be on the toad list. You might have posters of toads on your wall. They might be great actors and beautiful hunks of manhood, but they would be terrible husbands. Often, you could ask his last two wives. So it is important to know how to recognize a good-looking toad and pass him by.

Chapter 3

Once a Toad
Always a Toad?

CAN A TOAD become a prince? Absolutely. Any toad can become a prince. I have a number of wonderful friends who are great men to be around, excellent dads and husbands—quite princely; yet they were not always this way. Since I met them later in life, I never knew them as toads. They tell me stories about how awful they used to be, and I would have never guessed that they had once been total toads. How could you ever predict which toads will transform and which toads are toads for life? It is impossible. Many influences could cause a guy to change significantly. A spiritual transformation, a major tragedy or life event, simply growing up, or a woman's influence are all factors that could cause a notable change in a guy.

Female Rescuers

Although some guys have straightened out their lives because of a woman, it is always dangerous to date or marry a guy with the hopes of changing him into a prince or the man you want. The odds are not in your favor and you can be seriously hurt in the process. Don't be one of the well-meaning girls who thinks she can beat the odds. Many compassionate and naïve women sacrifice their own lives in an attempt to rescue the troubled man. Although a noble gesture, you can waste a lot of your prime time on these guys and you have no way to know if any changes you see in him are genuine. If he changes his life for the good without your help, you can be more confident that the change is real and permanent.

Lots of toads exist. You can be overwhelmed, discouraged, and injured if you waste your time on them. You need to efficiently sift through these distracting undesirables so you can spend your important time getting to know the princes.

> "The role of the female in every species is to pick the right mate. The wrong males are supposed to be barred from mating and procreating. Nature didn't intend human females or females from any other species to 'fix' deficient mates; we're just supposed to reject them so they don't pass on their bad genes."
>
> —Elizabeth, thoughtsopinionsrants Blog

Chapter 4

True Confessions—
The Author Is a Fake!

A Vet?

I MUST MAKE my first confession. The cover of the book shows that I am Dr. Kenneth Ryan. This is true. I am a doctor, but I am not a psychologist or a PhD in human relations or sexuality. I am a veterinarian. My letters are DVM. Obviously, my degree has absolutely nothing to do with this book, but I hope it gave the book cover an extra shred of credibility to at least get you to read this far. I invested a lot of time and money for my degree, and I am glad to use it for both my veterinary career and to help convince you that I might know what I am talking about.

Question Authority, Including Mine

I have read so many misguided books and articles by "qualified" people that I am confident this book is at least as helpful as other contemporary advice. I hope you are not gullible enough to assume that a book, a magazine article, a research study, a survey, or an opinion, are automatically true because some guy with an impressive resume says it is so. You must personally think through whatever you read in this book or from other authorities to determine what is true. Only *you* will live with the consequences of your choices.

Even Less Qualified

Another qualification I am lacking—I was never a good dater. In fact, it was my own ineptitude that led to the evolution of my rational dating philosophy. I got tongue-tied talking to girls and women. I had near heart attacks calling to ask for a date and moments of terror deciding how/when/if to kiss the girl goodnight.

Eventually, though, I discovered that many ordinary normal guys were just as pathetic as I was. Some are smooth operators, but many guys (potential princes) are just awkwardly doing the best they can. Many of our standard dating traditions don't make much sense, but people plunge forward just like everyone else because they don't want to be different or they haven't thought about it rationally. Many people find dating to be more stressful than enjoyable.

If you are intimidated or awkward with your current dating style, I hope to give you a fresh and encouraging perspective.

A Few Real Qualifications

I do have a few bonafide credentials that make me qualified to write this book. I have been happily married (most of the time) for over twenty years. My wife, Ruth, and I do premarital sex counseling for engaged couples. We have observed many couples and marriages over the years and almost without exception, the happiest and healthiest long-term relationships are those that followed many of the principles I share in this book.

On the other hand, I have seen people severely injured by relationships as they become attracted, fall in love, break up, and move on with another layer of scars from the betrayal, abuse, lies, and the overall pain of a break-up.

I have three daughters who are in their teenage years, so I have spent my life surrounded by women learning how they process life differently than I do.

I believe the wisdom of the quote in the introduction: "No decision you make in life will affect your future happiness or misery more than the choice of who you marry." The idea for this book occurred through conversations with my daughters about relationships. I started writing down many of the concepts that I thought they would want to know about boys and finding a good husband.

Why would a woman want relationship advice or insight from a man? Why would daughters want to know what their dad thinks? Because no woman knows the mind of a man better than a man. Men do not generally reveal the inner workings of our minds when it comes to sex and relationships. Young men especially do not care to reveal all that is on their minds. Other women can take their best shot at explaining male behavior, but they are not working from first hand experience. I can take you on a behind-the-scenes tour of the male mind.

I learned these bits of wisdom by my own trial and error, observations of life, and research. I want to pass this insight on to my children so they do not have to learn it the hard way. You are invited to listen in to nothing but straight talk.

Chapter 5

A Skull Full of Mush

MY MIND WAS mush as I started to fall in love with Ruth. I was lovesick, unable to concentrate, and distracted. I experienced butterflies in my stomach, excessive daydreaming, and euphoria. These are some of the symptoms of "falling in love." They are not imaginary responses; they are absolutely real. Chemicals in the brain actually change as a person enters into an exciting love relationship.

Paper Chase is a classic movie about students making it through law school. John Houseman, the intimidating, demanding professor, tells his students on the first day of class, "You come in here with a skull full of mush; you'll leave thinking like a lawyer." However, when each of those brilliant lawyer brains started falling in love, they turned back to mush. It is an inescapable law of humanity.

It is important to know about this law so that you can do some important thinking about relationships *before* your mind starts to go soft. Unfortunately, most people don't think very far ahead. They don't have a plan. They roll along with their feelings which are fun and exhilarating, but not the most reliable guide for life. Love, after all, is not supposed to be planned. It is spontaneous. Right? If you toss your road map out the window and decide you will rely on your feelings and spontaneity to get you to your destination, I predict you will make some wrong turns. Some will even end up in dangerous alleys.

I hope you are reading this book while you are not in love. I think I have a much better chance of convincing you of these truths if your mind is not already mushy. Most of my arguments are based on non-romantic logic. Once you are in the middle of a relationship, you may be less receptive to rational advice. If you think you can withstand the forces that have taken couples down since the beginning of time, you are naïve. If I have succeeded in persuading you to approach your relationship in a new way, it is important to make your plan or personal standards while you are in your right, logical, mush-free mind.

Chapter 6

Roadkill

Dead Opossum in the Middle of the Road

IN THE WORLD of road kill, opossums appear to be about the worst when it comes to safely crossing the road; however, I suspect that there are a number of "wise" opossums who tell their homely, hairy friends how easy it is to cross the road because they have successfully crossed the road themselves. Their instructions would be, "Just go to the side of the road and walk across. Fast or slow, no big deal, no need to check for traffic." However, thousands of road kill opossum carcasses suggest that there might be more to crossing the road than the wise opossums describe. In this case, the "wise" ones were just lucky enough to cross the road when no cars were coming so they honestly believe that their advice is good. I would suggest that every opossum would extend its ugly little lifespan if it looked both ways before crossing the street.

I will admit that I sometimes read about other couples, often celebrity couples, who have lived together happily for years, contradicting the dire effects that I claim will result from living together and sleeping together before marriage. I just read about a popular actress whom I admire on screen and off. She seems to have her act together and has been living with her boyfriend for the last four years. The fact that many people who slept together seem to be in a happy marriage or relationship does not change my recommendations at all. I am certainly happy for anyone

21

who has found their love of a lifetime, but their success does not mean that their methods are safe or usually effective.

If you interviewed a lottery winner, they might describe how they chose the winning numbers using their old high school locker number and their lucky grandmother's birthdate. Their millionaire status and number selection methods are undeniable but I would not advise anyone to drop out of college and start buying lottery tickets as a career choice. Instead, I would suggest that they visit with the 23 million people who used their lucky locker number but somehow failed to win their millions.

Regarding successful "living together" couples:

1. Some people dodge the bullet and are genuinely happy.
2. Some people are still in the honeymoon phase and rocky times are ahead.
3. Some people have deep scars from their past relationships that they do not reveal to anyone, particularly the *People* magazine interviewer or casual friends.

Let's check back with the happy couples in ten years.

In the meantime, I would still like to warn my fellow opossums to "look both ways before crossing." There are many life-altering relationship mistakes waiting to run you over like an oncoming truck. We do not want to find your emotions and self-esteem flattened in the middle of the road.

Chapter 7

The Plan—So Simple, So Powerful

IF YOU WERE a couch potato and decided that you wanted to run a 5K or a marathon, you would need to make some definite plans that would require a change in your actions in order to achieve that goal. If you do not make plans and follow through on them, it is unlikely that you will enjoy much success on the day of your big race. In fact, if you make no plans at all, you could miss the event entirely. Whether your goal is to run a marathon, make a batch of chocolate chip cookies, become a doctor, or become happily married, every goal or dream needs a rational plan in order to be achieved. Luck, chance, and incorrect information are unlikely to help achieve anything of significance.

Three Step Plan—Start All Three Today

1. **Learn to talk with guys.** More accurately, learn to *communicate* with guys. Your power lies here. No matter how pathetic you are at conversation, conversing is a learned skill and you can become an expert if you choose.

2. **Don't sleep with him**. This is the most common and most damaging mistake women make. First you must decide if abstinence until marriage will truly be your standard. The hard

part is actually sticking with your convictions. Simply deciding is not enough; you need a realistic plan.

3. **Don't panic**. Many women toss rational thinking to the wind because they fear that they will never find a man and be eternally lonely.

Remember these basics and I will proceed to fill in the details.

Section Two

LEARN TO TALK WITH GUYS

Chapter 8

Communication—
Your Most Important Skill

ONE OF THE top predictors of divorce relates to a couple's ability or inability to communicate with each other, especially in areas in which you disagree. Your efforts to learn how to talk with guys will pay off in all areas of your life including your search for a husband and later in your marriage. Wives who ask their husband every day, "How was your day?" are destined to get, "Fine," as their daily answer. Alternatively, women who have made the effort to learn how to communicate with men will know how to initiate and maintain meaningful conversations and thus enjoy their time more with their date or husband. The strength of your marriage will hang on your ability as a couple to communicate well during your good times and especially during your disagreements. Good communication is all about skills you can learn, it's not about your innate personality. This section will just scratch the surface and will serve to simply get you started.

Communication is such a large and important topic, you must commit to follow through with some of the referenced materials if you hope to improve your communication skills. Ultimately, you must step out and put your skills to use. Many women feel a sense of helplessness when they have few male prospects. Improving your skills is something you can do actively right now, and it can make a huge difference in your confidence and enjoyment of people around you. Let's get started!

> "What counts in making a happy marriage is not so much how compatible you are, but how you deal with incompatibility."
>
> —Leo Tolstoy

Chapter 9

Lips—Your Secret Weapon

"Ultimately the bond of all companionship, whether in marriage or
in friendship, is conversation."

—Oscar Wilde

MOST MEN HAVE a common weakness that plays directly into one of
your greatest strengths as a female. It is not your charm or your beauty,
but rather your ability and propensity to talk. Research suggests that

women tend to speak about twice as many words a day as men. Girls generally love to talk in social situations. Guys like to do things to avoid talking. Complete sentences are a bonus in many male conversations. Women gathered as friends can happily chat the night away. Men need a football game to stimulate conversation. Exceptions do exist.

Conversation is where your power as a woman lies. In fact, this weapon will give you as much influence as all the others combined. Here is the secret. Many boys and men are pathetic at conversation. We are frightened by it and try to avoid it. We get nervous worrying about what we will say. We get nervous *thinking* about calling a girl for a date or going on a date because we do not want to babble on with inane conversation or worse yet, sit in agonizing silence while our mind races for something to say. If you are able to put us at ease and encourage us to talk about things that are of interest to us, we will enjoy your company.

> *Conversation is where your power as a woman lies.*

You may be saying, *Sure I am a woman, but I can get stressed in social situations too.* Yes, that might be you today; however, with just a little effort, you can overcome this little weakness. You already have the tools—words. You like to talk and you are interested in relationships, not just male/female relationships, but all relationships. Most women are intuitively interested in how the people around them are relating. Other students, coworkers, and relatives all seem interesting to you. We guys, on the other hand, are often oblivious to the subtleties of the people around us. We are much more focused on ourselves and what we want or think. Obviously this is a gross generalization, but I think it is a valid point in simplified form.

Conversation is a rather odd topic in that it is one of the most important skills a person needs in order to navigate in this society, yet it is rarely taught or even discussed. There are fundamental principles of conversation that some people gradually figure out and they become good and comfortable with conversing, but for the vast majority of people, the thought of starting a conversation and keeping it going can make their palms sweat. It doesn't have to be this way. With a little knowledge and practice, you can talk easily with anyone, anywhere, about anything. Communication is the key to connecting with guys, getting to know them, enjoying their company, and evaluating your compatibility.

Teaching the art of conversation is too much for this book; however, I am going to give you an assignment and yes, there will be a test. You must buy or borrow a book called *Conversationally Speaking* by Alan Garner, which is the best book I have read on this topic. You will learn how to start a conversation and keep it going, how to extend an invitation that is likely to be accepted, how to mingle gracefully in a crowd, and how to disclose information about yourself in an interesting way. Confidence in this area will dramatically reduce your stress in dating as well as many other aspects of life. (I get no royalties from recommending this book and have made it required reading for every member of my family.)

> "Anything worth doing is worth doing
> poorly … until you can do it well."
> —Zig Zigler

Important Points

1. **Conversation is a learned skill**. It is rarely taught, so most people are not very good at it. If you never had piano lessons, I would not expect you to be very good at the piano. If you never had a soccer coach, you probably don't know many of the skills and the strategy of the game. Likewise, if you have not learned the art of talking to anybody anywhere, I would expect you to be poor at it, and therefore probably uncomfortable talking with people in many situations.

2. **Conversation requires practice.** Your piano lessons and soccer coach would not make much progress with you if you never practiced. You can receive instruction, but you must do the thing yourself in order to get good at it and gain confidence. When the crucial moment occurs at a piano recital or a big game, you are ready because you have been practicing. The same holds true with conversation. When you have the opportunity to be lab partners with the guy you admire or are introduced to the

gentle and gorgeous brother of a friend, you can be friendly, confident, and find yourself talking easily with the guy.

3. **Communication is not just talking**. A conversation can be about facts and situations. A poor conversation can be filled with talking that is boring and leads nowhere. You could talk about the weather but who cares. Some people mistakenly think they are conversing when they are telling their stories and opinions. By eliminating awkward silences, they think they are doing well, but they are not. A good conversationalist finds topics about which the other person is interested in talking. Ultimately, you want to be talking about things that interest both of you. When you are understanding each other, actively listening and connecting, communication is taking place. To elevate talking to communication is an art, and you are to become "the artist."

Three Common Mistakes

1. **Brain Cramp.** You have a brain cramp and have no idea what to say, so you say nothing, hoping the guy will think of something to say. Maybe you manage one simple line and then panic because you don't know what to say next. This describes me and probably the majority of people.

2. **Babbling.** Understanding that talking and conversation are not the same thing, is important. Some people are great at filling silence with their yammering stories or opinions. The conversation might not include awkward silences, but no real communication is taking place. Most people find excessive talkers to be tedious before long. Initially, it might seem better than excruciating silence, but all that talk will wear thin very quickly. In true conversation you are alternately asking questions to discover more about the other person and gradually disclosing information about yourself. The balance is part of the art.

3. **Too much.** There is a current trend in which many women are assertively pursuing guys. Women become too forward and make the guy feel uncomfortable. It is not a good idea to chase guys, but I will talk about that elsewhere (see the upcoming

section entitled "Dogs Chase Cars"). I encourage you to initiate a conversation, but too much assertiveness can make you look desperate or easy. Keep it casual and friendly—never pushy.

You are striving to be intelligent, interesting, friendly, and especially easy to talk to. That is who you are to become. Regardless of your shyness, personality, beauty, or plain-ness, you can become exceptionally easy to talk to.

DILBERT: © Scott Adams/Dist. by United Feature Syndicate, Inc. Used by Permission

Some of the Basics

A smile and basic greeting break the silence and break the ice. Often, we don't do this because we are unsure of the next step.

One or two simple questions can get you started, but you need to probe with a few questions to figure out which way you could go with the conversation. You must find something in which the guy is interested. If you are lucky, early in the conversation you find a small piece of common ground in which you also have some interest.

Magic Open-ended Questions

For me, the first questions that enter my mind are usually dead end (closed-ended) questions like, "Are you enjoying the game?", "What is your major?" or "How long have you worked here?" They all have one word answers. These are OK to break the ice and at least establish contact, but if you string together too many one-word-answer questions you will sound like an FBI interrogator. The magic lies with open-ended questions. They invite the person to answer in complete sentences and you gain back much more information that you can use in the conversation. Open-ended questions would be like these: "Why do you like playing football?" "How did you find such an interesting job?" "Tell me what you guys say in a huddle."

There are a few important guidelines to know, but this is really not too difficult. For instance, don't ask questions that are too open-ended such as, "Tell me about yourself." (I know it is a statement, but for conversation it counts as a question.) Wide-open questions are overwhelming since the person has no idea where to start or how much to say. Open-ended questions begin with these words: why, how, tell me, and in what way. Closed-ended questions start with these words: are, do, who, when, where, and which. The word "what" can be open or closed-ended.

The book I recommended earlier, *Conversationally Speaking*, is not long or difficult. Just read a chapter and start to practice on anyone. Then when the moment arrives and you want to talk to a guy, you will be all practiced up and you won't squander the opportunity. Until you start to talk with the guy, you are just one more face in the crowd, but if you are one of the easiest girls to talk to that he ever met, you have his attention.

Right now conversations with new people may seem as scary and unrealistic as you performing a violin recital tonight. If you decide it is important, read the book and practice. You will reap the rewards in romance and all parts of your life. You can do it!

> When marrying, ask yourself this question:
> Do you believe that you will be able to converse well
> With this person into your old age?
> Everything else in marriage is transitory.
> —Friedrich Nietzsche

Chapter 10

Practice on Someone You Don't Care About

NOBODY STARTS OUT as an expert conversationalist. Many of us are especially intimidated by the opposite sex. You might be a perfectly normal, engaging woman until you are faced with a man in whom you might have some interest. Then, to your exasperation, your mind goes absolutely blank at the moment of truth. You both fumble for casual conversation. You replay the encounter in your mind for the rest of the day, stunned at the stupid remarks you made. Hours later you think of all the things you wish you had said.

What You Need Is Practice

You need practice being around guys and talking with them. The best guys to practice on are the safe, non-threatening guys who you don't care about. If you don't care, the pressure is off. (Note: "someone you don't care about" refers only to anyone who is not a prospective relationship partner. They are still people who deserve respect and real conversation. They are not experimental pawns.) These guys may be young or old, slightly geeky, or very plain. If asked out by one of these types, your first impulse might be to schedule a root canal. They clearly do not appear in any of your dreams about husbands. Why would you want to waste your time? What if people see you talking with this guy? What if he likes you and asks you out? How will you shake him?

35

These questions are all excellent. You are a likable person and there is a chance he will become interested in you. No problem. I'll help you with that possible problem in an upcoming section entitled "How to Dump a Guy Humanely"; however, you are *not* wasting your time. You are practicing purposely on non-spouse material so you will be more experienced and ready when you come across real spouse material. Most people are nervous in new situations, so it will be helpful to gain this social experience when the game is not on the line. Immature women might give you some grief for talking with a "loser," but guys either won't care or they may even be impressed. Meanwhile, you will be gaining experience in extended one-on-one conversation with a guy.

When I worked as a camp counselor during my college summers, I saw a couple of very attractive, outgoing twins who were young counselors. They had cheerleader looks and confidence, but they treated all the boys, whether nerds or jocks, with kindness and respect. It really grabbed my attention to see them being kind to guys who would normally get the instant brush off from fashionable girls like themselves.

To clarify, don't waste your time if you already know that the guy's a total toad. Total toad status would disqualify him from being a safe person to talk with. Practice on the guys who may have some social rough edges, but are essentially safe and non-intimidating. Actually, you can practice on anyone, any sex, and any age. The techniques are the same and the more you practice, the better you will become.

For example, while standing in line with strangers you would normally ignore, try saying something to establish some sort of contact. Give yourself a personal challenge that on your next shopping outing, you will smile and say hello to at least three people—any people. Then, try following up that hello with a question or comment that will encourage the other person to respond to you. This is a huge step that many people never try but it is critical if you want to make relational contact with the world around you and eventually make new friends—possibly even a guy friend. In order for two strangers to become friends, someone must say "hello." If you spend your life waiting for the other person to say hello, you will miss many opportunities for friendships.

The way you smile and say hello to a fifty-year-old woman sitting beside you on a bus will be almost the same as the smile and hello you give to the guy you would like to meet. You do not need to be flirtatious, witty, or aggressive. Just smile and talk with the person in a relaxed, friendly way. Women who can do this are so uncommon that you will capture the guy's attention without coming on too strong.

I expect that the frightening part of this plan is what to say after "hello." That frightens me too; in fact, that frightens almost everyone. That is why it sets you apart so distinctly if you are able to say something intelligent next. This is why it's worth the effort to get the *Conversationally Speaking* book. Learn it. Practice it. Make it part of your life. Don't stress over the personality you were born with; simply gain the skills you need and continually improve. If you are able to routinely make conversation with almost anyone, you will have confidence and poise when you meet a man of interest.

I am an introvert so my natural tendency is to keep to myself. I expend a lot of mental energy when I must talk with people; therefore, I do not want to talk with every person I see, and I don't feel obligated to do so. As I have developed conversation skills, though, I have found that I can make a conscious decision about talking with someone or not. If I decide to make the first contact and perhaps engage in a conversation, I can do it comfortably. I used to be horribly awkward and intimidated; now I can usually do it when I choose. My personality did not change; only my skills changed. I am confident that you can overcome your fear and make great progress if it is important to you.

If loneliness is a challenging issue for you, the ability to establish contact is a basic skill you must master in order to have a life filled with good friends. Make your embarrassing mistakes on people you may never see again or who are not critically evaluating your social style. Whether you meet a guy, make a friend, or just improve your social skills, practice, practice, and practice some more on anyone.

Chapter 11

Smile

MY WIFE AND I recently saw "The Little Mermaid" on Broadway. Before the show, several people were selling programs. One young woman was selling more programs than anyone else because she had a great technique. She held her programs high and used her natural smile to radiate warmth and enthusiasm. After watching her for awhile, I was certain that the smile was not entirely natural. Her smile was certainly genuine, but I believe she was smiling with a purpose. Perhaps she had taught herself to smile as needed. Whenever someone purchased a program, her smile shifted to a pleasant look as she made change. When the transaction was over, she would lift up the program, look out, and smile again. I observed her pattern. She was simply turning on the smile and it worked. She was totally engaging. People wanted to respond to her.

Few things enhance a woman's attractiveness as much as an engaging smile. Most people, if given the option, would choose to talk with a smiling person over a non-smiling; therefore, why not choose to be the smiler?

Smiles come more easily for some than for others, but anyone can learn to smile. If you are not a natural smiler, you will need to work on it. We can all recognize a fake smile so it is important to make your smile real. Your eyes must smile along with your mouth. Hopefully, you already know how to smile and simply need to remind yourself to do it

> *Few things
> enhance a woman's
> attractiveness
> as much as an
> engaging smile.*

more often—especially in situations where you might be hoping to be in conversation with a guy.

Just as you can practice your conversation skills on anyone (especially people you do not care about romantically), you can also practice your smile any time. The more you do it, the more quick and ready it will be. Meanwhile, you will make the world a friendlier place.

Be careful, though. Too much of a smile can make you seem overly forward or flirtatious and will cause the guy to move away. I am suggesting a friendly-flight-attendant type smile.

Smile with Your Eyes

In the privacy of your own room, you can practice your smile in the mirror. Be sure no one is around since it could be humiliating. Check your eyes and eyebrows. Your eyes may be even more essential than your mouth to achieve a warm, genuine smile. The action of smiling with your eyes is difficult to describe, but we all know it when we see it. Your cheekbones and eyebrows shift unconsciously and somehow create a subtle twinkle or "lighting up." During a true spontaneous smiling moment, the changes happen naturally. If you study your face in the mirror you can learn to flash the real deal smile almost whenever you choose.

When you are in front of your mirror, cover your mouth with a piece of paper so you can concentrate on your eyes. Move the paper and play around with it to smile with just your mouth or just your eyes or both. The adjustments are so subtle, I cannot tell you exactly how to do it, but you will recognize your own smiling eyes when you see them. When you find the right look, repeat it and try to remember which muscles are working and what you did. This is how you can turn your unconscious actions into conscious ones. Try holding the smile a little longer than normal to exercise your smile muscles. Some people have great long term smiles, but many smiles are flashed more than held. When the photographer takes too long to snap the picture, my smile turns into a hideous plastic grin. I am only able to flash a true smile for limited time.

Embarrassing Tip

I have often used this little trick just before meeting someone I want to impress. Use it with caution; don't get caught. Just before opening the door to meet your date, open your mouth as wide as you can (like you are about to swallow a whole apple) and raise your eyebrows as high as possible. You will look like you are about to be hit by a bus. Hold this position for a few seconds, and then relax. Your smiling muscles will be warmed up and you will feel slightly ridiculous which leaves a residual half smile on your face. The person you are about to meet has no idea how your face was contorted two seconds before the door opened. He only knows that you look pleasant and happy to see him. Try it. It works.

Smile First, Happy Second

Normally we think we smile when we are happy. The process can work in reverse. Think a pleasant thought and force the smile when you are not happy and you may begin to feel happier.

Whatever your smile aptitude, you will benefit if you commit to finding your best smile and using it more often. Practice when you don't need to be smiling so it comes naturally when you do.

Chapter 12

High School Strategy

"I'M 17 AND I still haven't been on a date" is a common high school lament. Many girls in high school spend a lot of time worrying because they have not been pursued by any boys. It would be a comforting validation if *someone* were interested. If *no* one is interested, a young girl might decide she is not worthy of a guy or that she will never find a husband.

Time to Ripen

Most high school boys have no idea who they are or what they are about. They are starting to seriously work those thoughts out, but they are usually not there yet. At the same time, their hormones are surging and taking over brain functions. Obviously then, high school is not the best time to be picking your man. Give them a little more time to ripen.

While the high school guys are growing up, you can hone your own interactive skills. You have the chance to be around all kinds of guys. Figure out how to talk to them, how to have fun with them, and how to make them comfortable with your easy conversation. These concepts are not easy. It takes practice, but it will prepare you for the future when you are around guys who really might be prince material. In a few years, you will have refined your approach. You will not be afraid to talk to that possible prince and he is more likely to recognize you as the sort of girl he enjoys being with; therefore, group activities, non-romantic double dates (just fun), service projects, etc. all give you a chance to be around boys. Work on the school play, participate in the band, serve in student government, or involve yourself in a club. Make mistakes. Be clumsy. Learn and press on. Everybody has situations that cause you to bury your face in a pillow when you get home and cry, "I can't believe I just said that." The stupid thing you uttered keeps replaying in your brain. These are all mistakes you can live with. The mistakes you make on a romantic date and with a boyfriend tend to have much greater consequences. Make small mistakes now to prevent large mistakes later.

When you are in high school, it seems like the world is very small and limited to those kids in your class. Lots of high schoolers, including myself, worried a lot about peer pressure and how the other students perceived them. You will probably end up like most people, though, and high school will become ancient history the day you walk off the stage with your diploma. If you go off to college, you get a fresh start with people who couldn't care less how popular or unpopular you were in high school. The prom might have seemed like the most important event in the world at the time, but one month later, you'll find it is irrelevant.

If you are not college bound, you will find that the working world also does not care if you were a high school star or a nobody. Now, the world sizes you up for exactly who you are.

After high school, guys are more likely to have a reality check and they start making decisions about which way they will go in life. Many of the geeks grow in confidence and begin to look like nice, normal people with whom you might want to associate. Many of the stars have found that no one cares about their high school successes. Cheerleader, football star, and class president credentials don't impress anyone a year later. High school resumes are like monopoly money. They seem important during the game, but in real life, they don't mean much. Your character and integrity are what matter most now.

So, give the high school guys a chance to grow up before even considering pairing off with one of them. This determination will give you tremendous freedom and peace of mind. You do not have to feel like a loser because you have not gone out on a date. If you interact with guys and learn to discern the princes from the toads, you are right on schedule. You are in the game with full participation.

As you get older, some of the rules will change; however, many will remain the same.

There are exceptions to these rules. I would not want my daughters forced into some perfect progression of life relationships. I am not smart enough to create the perfect mold, so, I am only throwing these out as suggested guidelines. One of my best friends in high school got married the summer we graduated from high school. Most of us thought he was crazy, but they have been happily married for twenty-seven years and have no regrets. In their case, I am glad they did not follow my advice. They were the exception to the rule. Another friend reports that of six high school classmates married right out of high school, all are now divorced. Those are tough odds.

Chapter 13

Fateful Attraction

WHAT MAKES ONE person attracted to another? Nobody knows. Attraction can be a troublesome issue for singles because so often the guy you are attracted to is not interested in you, and unfortunately, you will have guys attracted to you in whom you have no romantic interest. We do not know a lot about attraction, but a few characteristics are undeniable and important to understand.

1. Attraction cannot be forced
2. Attraction cannot be faked (long term)
3. Attraction CAN be influenced

Virtually all women want to be attractive, but the standard for beauty changes over time. For example, in old paintings, naked ladies often appear a bit plump and motherly, which was the sexy look in the 1600s. More current trends picture beauty as exceptionally skinny supermodels and overbusted centerfolds. Women go to great lengths with diets, plastic surgery, exercise, and other extreme measures to make themselves look like the expected beauty standard. Some of these measures may have an effect, but ultimately, no matter how much you want a man to like you, you cannot force attraction. It's like trying to push a rope—it just doesn't work, so don't waste your time trying to force the issue.

Likewise, it is fruitless for anyone to pretend to be attracted to another person. You wouldn't want either of you to fake it. If you are to be a couple, you need the magic of genuine mutual attraction. Finding this might take awhile, but it will be worth the wait.

Some predictability regarding who is attractive can be found at the upper end of the scale. Some women have facial features and bodies that would be instantly recognized as beautiful by both men and women. However, most people fall into the more ordinary "average looks" category. Average looking people are not attractive to everyone. Fortunately, a very wide spectrum of men exist with varied tastes. You do not need to be attractive to everyone. You just need to be attractive to one.

Three Ways That Men Are Attracted to Women

1. **General Physical Attraction**—A combination of body shape, face, hair, etc. combine to create the overall look that somehow makes a man think a woman is attractive. There is tremendous variability in personal preferences.
2. **Sexual Attraction**—Nakedness, short skirts, cleavage, enticing movement, exposed skin, clothing associated with sexual attraction, and more combine to exude sexual attraction.
3. **Personality Attraction**—Whatever makes people like you and want to be with you regardless of the way you look is personality attraction. Included in this category are your character, integrity, inner beauty, sense of humor, kindness, etc.

General Physical Attraction

Many unpredictable factors are at work when it comes to physical attraction: some you can influence, some you can't. A healthy and sane approach concerning our looks helps us do what we can to enhance areas we can change and not fret about things we cannot change. Many women become obsessed with their appearance, and there are certainly some obvious measures which you can take to improve your appearance. The top three over which you have control are:

1. **Weight:** If you are overweight, check with your doctor to determine if you have a medical problem. If not, your weight is your decision.
2. **Hair:** Men notice hair. Find a style that you like. Some face shapes are complemented by different hair styles.
3. **Make up:** Done right, almost every woman looks better with makeup. Subtle is usually better. Ask for advice from a woman you admire. Most women would be flattered and honored if you sought their help because you think they do makeup very well. Have fun experimenting with different looks. Remember though, keep it subtle.

Do what you can to enhance your appearance, but be content with who you are.

Sexual Attraction

Sexual attraction includes cleavage, nakedness, body curves, and attitude. Sexual attraction is distinctly different from general attraction. A guy can look into your pretty eyes and be mesmerized without thinking about sex. Sexual attraction is from the neck down and stimulates at least fleeting thoughts of sex in the guy. Sex is an effective, superficial attractant for most males; however, the males who are willing to pursue a female based entirely on this attraction will probably be poor choices for boyfriends or husbands. Chasing sexy women will be a hard pattern to break. If sexiness was his sole reason for pursuing you, he will surely see other sexy women who will be enticing. Eventually this type of shallow man will find someone sexier than you, and he will move on to his next conquest; therefore, I do not recommend trying to enhance this type of attraction. The guys you catch will be throwaways. Many women, however, use sexual attraction because it works and they are desperate.

Personality Attraction

Personality is the most ignored aspect of attraction, but it is actually the most important. It is part of the common joke, "She has a great personality" which means she is not physically attractive. Personality attraction is much more important for lifetime compatibility than the other two types of attraction. Personality attraction can significantly influence how a man views your physical attractiveness. A man's general physical attraction to a female can shift based on attraction to her personality.

Cinderella's Prince

In the Cinderella musical, the prince sings, "Do I love you because you're beautiful or are you beautiful because I love you?" Great question, Prince. Often guys cannot sort out the difference in their own minds—even if they want to. All they know is that they are attracted. That is why evaluating a relationship can be so confusing. If he loves you only because you are beautiful, you may be in trouble if you put on a few pounds or start your bulges and sags too soon in your marriage. If he finds you beautiful because he loves you, this attraction is just as genuine and effective as attraction from innate physical beauty. Mutual physical attraction is a critical element for a passionate marriage. You had better have it.

All of this matters because your physical attractiveness will decline as you age. If your relationship is built upon physical attraction and sexual attraction without much personality attraction, you might be in trouble when your appearance changes. Personality attraction, however, can get stronger and stronger as you grow together. Thankfully, we are wired so that even we average looking people have a good chance of being attractive to someone if we have an attractive personality.

You Are Not Trapped

You are not trapped by your personality. You can be anyone you choose. I'm not suggesting that you try to fake a personality or pretend to be someone you are not. I encourage you to grow and improve yourself. If you are naturally shy, you can learn to talk with people even though conversation does not come easily to you. The traits and skills described in this section can be learned and developed by anyone. However, you will need to do more to learn how. It is too much for this book. Your personality will attract a man who truly appreciates the inner you. These communication skills are equally important in marriage or singleness so it is worth the effort to start developing them now.

Interestingly, Ben Franklin was a brilliant, multitalented social man. He had a lot going for him, yet he made lists of personality traits that he wanted to improve and systematically went about trying to do so. If Ben had room for improvement, we probably do too.

Are You Safe?

Guys need to feel safe around you. They want to be themselves and not feel like they must perform or present a false front. Cutting remarks, even in jest, are not endearing. Speaking poorly of others makes a man wonder if you will speak poorly of him. If you are safe to be with, you will be more attractive to the man who interests you.

Important Note

If the guy is not initially attracted to you and feels like you are manipulating the situation to get him to like you, he may actually become repulsed. Remember, you cannot force attraction. If you are caught blatantly flirting, it is embarrassing, ineffective, and frustrating. A neutral but friendly attitude is comfortable for both. If he starts to feel attraction, he will send signals and you can respond to them. If he is not attracted, there is nothing you can do but stay friendly. Eventually, you will find a person who is mutually attracted to you.

Chapter 14

The Beauty Curse

MANY AVERAGE LOOKING girls grow up watching the "in" crowd of beautiful people, wishing they had their looks and popularity. Ironically, life will be much easier for you if you are only moderately attractive. "Moderate" covers a very wide range. In fact, you can be thankful if you are among the masses of very average looking women.

> *Ironically, life will be much easier for you if you are only moderately attractive.*

Beauty is not all in the eye of the beholder. There are some girls who are inherently beautiful. You could show a photo of these beauties to 100 males and every single guy would be drawn to them. Knowing nothing else about them except how they look, men would want to see them in person, talk to them, brush by them, touch them, get to know them, and probably sleep with them. Guys would act like moths to a porch light. That is the way males are wired to respond to beauty.

Perhaps you should have sympathy rather than envy for the beauties. The good news for that pretty girl is that she can at least get the attention of virtually every guy just because of her looks. She has the largest field of possibilities in choosing the guys in whom she is interested. The bad news is that often, the less desirable of those guys are the ones clamoring most aggressively for her attention—likely blocking her view from some of the less confident but much more desirable guys. She may spend much of her single life having to clear away the undesirables so she is available to the choice guys. Her problem is that many of those undesirables are very good at surface traits. They look good, move with confidence, and say what she wants to hear. The pretty girl gets sucked in because she is totally unaware of the game being played. She wants to think she has it under control, but most girls grossly underestimate the sexual nature of boys. As I have said, I have been in locker rooms as boys discuss girls. Most girls would and should be appalled by the way girls are discussed—especially the prettiest girls. The undesirable males especially like to discuss the pretty girls and the girls who have been deceived to put out their sexuality. The average girls are more likely to be left alone. Remember, the object is to find one very good man, not dozens of mediocre men.

What should you do if you happen to be high on the beauty scale? Do not accentuate and magnify your beauty too much. You can wear modest clothes and moderate makeup and the boys will still notice you. Regardless of the fashion that is in style when you are reading this, if you wear tight blouses, short skirts, tight skirts, or low-cut shirts, you will push the guys over the edge. They cannot help but look at you—every one of them. If you are beautiful and wear attention-grabbing clothes, you can guarantee you will be discussed by the undesirables. You can reduce the unwanted clutter of males around you by toning down your look. The desirable princes will recognize your beauty even in a sweatshirt. One day, you will be able to unleash all of your sizzle on your husband who will treasure and respect every beautiful inch of you. In the meantime, keep your sizzle away from guys who don't deserve it.

You are thinking, *Thankfully, I was spared from being beautiful.* Probably not.

The Late Bloomer Blessing

I have looked at Ruth's high school yearbook picture in which she had braces, long straight hair, and average looks. She could have been a future librarian. No one, including me, would have paused on her page to admire that senior picture, but by the time I saw her at Michigan State University, I thought she was beautiful. What had changed? Yes, she had blossomed physically, but at the same time, she had been developing an inner beauty and great character because she did not grow up with a sense that she was particularly pretty. She was just average in looks but exceptional in character. Thankfully, she was preserved for me. She was 27 when we were married.

A woman's beauty begins to rise in the eyes of a man when he finds he enjoys her company. He realizes he can be himself without needing to put up a false front. Conversation seems easy. For some reason, he never worries about what to say or moments of silence when he is with her. If her character creates that kind of response, her beauty is enhanced in his eyes.

Inner beauty is real. A woman of beautiful character becomes genuinely more attractive to a man of high character.

Inner beauty is real. A woman of beautiful character becomes genuinely more attractive to a man of high character. The relationship may or may not blossom into romantic attraction, but quality character has an unquestionably positive effect.

Chapter 15

Dogs Chase Cars; Girls Chase Boys

Chasing Cars

IF YOU WATCH a dog chase a car you will notice a few things. He almost never catches the car, and if he does, he gets more than he bargained for. The car is not impressed with the dog. The dog enjoys the thrill of the chase but doesn't get anything from the car. The dog does all the work, and the driver usually ignores the dog. Sometimes drivers find the dog annoying and sometimes the dog gets run over.

Girls chasing boys is about as effective as dogs chasing cars. Dogs never catch the car and girls who chase boys rarely catch a keeper. Just as a dog enjoys the chase, a girl might enjoy the thrill of the chase but she is doing all the work. The car driver might ignore the dog, be annoyed by the dog, or run over the dog and a boy is likely to do the same things when chased by a girl. Boys often find aggressive girls to be annoying. Ultimately, he might allow himself to be caught long enough to run her over, taking advantage of her desperation and causing serious hurt. Girls have a better chance of catching their quarry than the dog catching a car; however, aggressive pursuit creates an unfavorable dynamic in a relationship and many unexpected consequences result if you set your sights on a guy and go after him.

Chasing Boys

The trend seems to be that girls are getting more aggressive in their pursuit of boys, which is usually not a good idea. You have probably noticed that you appreciate things you work for more than things that are just handed to you. If you decided you wanted a bike when you were a young girl and worked odd jobs to earn money for it, the day you bought it was a big day. You would take extra good care of it because you knew how hard you worked to get it. The effort you put into earning it adds to your appreciation of the bike. On the other hand, if your rich uncle buys you a brand new state-of-the-art bike every six months, you will probably be more careless with it because you got it with no effort. It is a better bike than the one you could have bought for yourself, yet it has a lower value in your eyes. Assigning a perceived value to things around us is a trait of human nature and it applies equally in the world of relationships.

If a guy gets the girl too easily, her value is diminished in his eyes. He may still agree to be with you, but his respect for you is inherently lowered. Girls who pursue boys appear desperate. You may think you are liberated and simply getting the boy you picked. Unfortunately, you are getting less than you bargained for. When I was single and generally striving to have noble intentions with girls, something clicked in my mind if a girl was pursuing me. Somehow, I thought I might get more from her because she obviously couldn't resist me and might be willing to pay some sort of price to get me. Even if I was not interested in her, I was curious about what she might be willing to do to get me. That should be a frightening message for you. I did not act on my impulses but the impulses were there. Remember, a key question about any guy, "What keeps him from acting on his impulses?" Be careful plotting your way to a guy since you can send the wrong message and fall into a habit of manipulation.

> *If a guy gets the girl too easily, her value is diminished in his eyes.*

Chapter 16

Flirting

THE DICTIONARY DEFINES *flirting* as "playful romantic or sexual overtures." This broad definition could include both actions that are perfectly okay and some that are not recommended. People flirt to indirectly communicate they have a heightened interest in the other person. One problem with flirting is that it is often overdone. Although the flirter may think she is being subtle, oftentimes she is more obvious than she knows. Other girls may find flirters to be obnoxious. Boys may or may not be responsive. If you come on too strong, you might look desperate and cheap.

Although some subtle flirting is normal and acceptable, I would suggest replacing flirting with conversation. By initiating a conversation or asking a few open-ended questions to extend a conversation, you can subtly communicate a heightened interest in the guy. By plunging a little beyond typical meaningless conversation, he may realize that talking with you was easy and enjoyable and he should be perceptive enough to notice that you were relaxed and enjoyed his company too. A connection such as this is all you could hope for in early contacts. You cannot force a guy to be attracted to you, so being yourself is important. He needs to be attracted to the real you if you are to have any future together. If he has a glimpse of your true character and has no interest, don't worry about it and don't try to force it. Gracefully and confidently move on.

Chapter 17

Chance Meetings

WHAT IF INTERESTING guys are too shy or passive to initiate? What can you do without chasing?

Although it is not a good idea to chase guys, there are subtle things you can do to help make contact. Go for the opportunity to be in his study group. Ask, "Can I join you?" if he's sitting alone at lunch. It would probably be comfortable for both of you if you can sit down and have a friendly, platonic conversation. If you are already acquainted, ask for help moving something or fixing something. Be genuine and subtle.

A Few Mistakes

1. **Too many chance meetings.** A guy will start to think something is up when you bump into him at the coke machine four days in a row.
2. **Illogical circumstances.** Sometimes in your eagerness to create some type of contact, you rationalize a bit too much. Perhaps you created some rational explanation for your actions when your actions really do not make much sense. Suddenly your true scheming intentions are obvious. How embarrassing!
3. **Obsession.** You can become obsessed with plotting to make contact. Perhaps you are not obviously chasing him, but you are

mentally chasing him. Your manipulations will probably become obvious. You may get in the habit of manipulating to get what you want which is an unhealthy and irritating characteristic.

4. **Stalking.** Don't get creepy.

I am sure you are creative enough to think of subtle actions to increase your odds of an encounter. The key, once again, is conversation. What you are really doing is creating a chance to talk with him. In one short conversation, you could find out enough about him to cross him off your list of guys in whom you could be interested. Otherwise, your hope is to have a reasonably comfortable conversation with him. Guys remember girls who are easy to talk to. At least you have broken the ice. Hopefully, you learned a little more about him that would help you when you get another chance to talk. If you are skilled at conversation you will be more relaxed with the confidence to be yourself.

Also, note that simply initiating a conversation might be considered flirting by some. If you try to be too clever or coy or flirtatious, your motives may be too obvious. Just strive for a normal, interesting platonic conversation.

In this department, you might do well to consult other women for tips. Ask some happily married women how they met their husbands. Some women are very clever and most enjoy talking about their man and how they met. Even your grandmother might surprise you with how she worked this magic on Grandpa.

Chapter 18

First Date

IN HIGH SCHOOL, I was a borderline geek. I got excellent grades and was socially awkward with girls, but I was good friends with a few of the popular athletes. By my senior year, I had never been on a date. Somehow word filtered down that if I asked out a friend of a friend, she would go out with me. Let's call her Cindy. I barricaded myself in my parents' bedroom where I could have a telephone with privacy and prepared to make my call. With my heart pounding, I dialed her number. I was strong on the first six numbers, but I couldn't quite bring myself to dial the last number. I hung up the phone, slumped in the chair, and breathed a huge sigh of relief that I was still safe and had not embarrassed myself yet. One or two rounds of phone fright is understandable. After that, a guy starts to feel like a loser. After a few more minutes, I solidly fit into the loser category, but I finally gathered all the courage of *Braveheart* and dialed all seven numbers. Cindy answered. I stammered a bit but managed to make my invitation. She easily agreed and the date was set. I was headed for my first date.

Cindy was cute. She was friendly and talked a lot, and she had a lot of experience at dating. I was very likely a mercy date. Perhaps she wanted to break in a borderline geek. I think we both knew that we were not really compatible. We ended up going out several times, and I started to learn for the first time all the good, bad, and ugly thoughts that go through a guy's mind on a date. As I dated sporadically in college and shot the bull with roommates, I came to understand that many male thoughts and responses are universal.

On that very first date with Cindy, she was an experienced dater and I a raw rookie. We kissed that first night—I mean really kissed. I was absolutely electrified. I had never experienced that kind of rush. I was definitely interested in another date. Actually, I was interested in another kiss. The date was just a means to the end. I already knew that I would never want to marry this girl for a number of reasons, but I was sure interested in kissing her. I wanted her lips; I was not too concerned about who was attached to the lips. It took us a few weeks to break things off in a friendly way. This was my first glimpse at how our judgment can be severely impaired by the pleasure that comes from sensual/sexual contact.

Chapter 19

Non-Dating

"Marriage, ultimately, is the practice of becoming
passionate friends."

—Harville Hendrix

BEFORE YOU GET into a more romantic relationship, you must
plan ahead if you want to be sure that you are compatible as friends;
otherwise, standard dating practices will automatically route you onto
the romantic couple track.

Why is it helpful to be friends before you are lovers? When you are
married, the majority of your life is spent doing ordinary daily activities
that have nothing to do with romance. Going to work, visiting friends
and family, changing diapers, fixing the house, paying bills: there's
absolutely nothing romantic about any of these. Mundane tasks are
much more tolerable if they are shared with someone who is your best
friend. The "good kisser" title is not much help when one of your kids
is throwing up in the middle of the night. The one percent of marriage
that is hugging, kissing, sex, and romance is automatically pleasurable. It
is the other 99% that becomes unbearable if you don't genuinely enjoy
doing lots of things with your spouse. Actually, if your 99% is not good,
your 1% will also be bad.

If you begin a relationship with a strong friendship and true compatibility, you may shift into a more serious relationship later if you choose.

Make Your First Date Stress-free (Almost)

Here is a way to make your first date more comfortable for both of you. When you receive the invitation, you could say something like this: "Thanks for thinking of me, Jason. I would really enjoy getting to know you better. You seem like a neat guy. I'm not really interested in a relationship right now, but I would love to go out with you as a friend. If that's okay with you, I would love to go to that concert." The goodnight kiss is eliminated and you are relieved of some of the pressure to impress each other.

Entering the date with these words positions you as just a couple of ordinary people getting together rather than a potential romantic couple. By contemporary dating standards, the outing is really sort of a non-date. Commitment is reduced for both the man and woman. Without the romantic expectations, you have a chance to evaluate the guy objectively. You can find out a lot about someone in a few hours of conversation and activity. If you see any red flags that would rule him out as a compatible mate, you are not in very deep. Having never advanced to dating status, it is so much easier on both of you to remain friends or acquaintances than to backtrack from romantic involvement. Less pressure on both of you to perform or impress the other. You are safer to be yourselves.

In some situations, the statement above might be more than you need. If you are already acquainted or you perceive that the guy is just inviting you to a friendly activity, you may not need to use the disclaimer statement and simply accept the invitation. Once on the date, you could bring up the subject in the course of your conversations. Discussing your general views of dating early in the relationship is an interesting and revealing topic of discussion. It is an indirect way to DTR (define the relationship) before either of you starts to get serious.

If you get even a little physical and the guy happens to be hot and a good kisser, you might be tempted to stay with him for awhile just for the excitement and pleasure. He might have a lot of very good qualities, but also enough annoying characteristics to show you that you would not enjoy doing a lot of real life activities with him. Yet, there you are as a couple for a while, wasting your time until the break up.

At first glance this might seem like an odd approach, especially if you really are craving a romantic relationship. You are not lying. In fact you are stating the truth. You are not interested in a romantic relationship until you have established a solid friendship. It makes sense that there can be certain times in a woman's life when she is not interested in a relationship. For instance, in high school she may be too busy with activities, her parents won't let her date, or she wants to concentrate on classes and getting into college. Later, a woman might be putting all her energy into college or her job and doesn't have time for a serious relationship. Perhaps she just broke up with a boyfriend and needs time to get over it. Maybe she is studying for the Bar exam or training for the Olympics.

Such situations are all very realistic. Few people would question the legitimacy of these reasons. You could be the hottest, most frequent dater in the world and still find a phase of your life when you "are not interested in a relationship right now."

In your case, simply adopt this boundary line as a full time policy. If you say it with conviction—as if this is only a temporary phase in your life—you can pull it off. No need to be embarrassed. You have bought yourself precious time to learn about the guy without all the emotional risk and stress of stepping into and out of a relationship. Get in. Get out. Nobody gets hurt.

You Might Change Your Mind

At any point in your future friendship, you have the option of telling the guy that you changed your mind and are starting to see him as more than just a friend. Even on the first date, you might end up discussing some of this to see how it floats. Setting clear boundaries provides both respect and safety.

Don't Try to Explain It on the Phone

This strategy is far too unique to try to explain during an initial invitation. That is why you give the simple, believable line and let it go. If the guy turns out to be a loser or at least not your type, you don't need to try to explain yourself, and he just thinks you are an overcommitted student.

From the Guy's Perspective

Almost every guy must work up the nerve to invite a girl out. For some, it is just a glimmer of stress, but for others, it is absolute terror. I used to dial six numbers and hang up before the seventh number, or take deep breaths and carefully plan my words. Yes, I was pathetic but certainly I was not alone. If a guy called you because he thinks you are cute or likeable, he is hoping there might be some kind of relationship, maybe just physical, but maybe he truly thinks you would be a great girlfriend or wife. His greatest fear is that you would say, "Get lost, loser."

Men are very sensitive to rejection. Anything short of outright rejection will probably be a relief. The fact that you enthusiastically agreed to go out with him will completely blot out the extra little detail that asserted you were "not interested in a relationship right now." He will assume that once you get to know him, you won't be able to resist. Almost any guy will be thrilled to get his foot in the door. If he is Mr. Right or at least a decent prince, he could be correct. You might be willing to move to a more serious relationship eventually if he is a great guy. You have bought yourself time to get to know him without getting tangled up emotionally or physically. Men of character can deal with boundaries.

On the Date, You Might Have to Remind Him

On the night of the date, this guy is probably on dating auto pilot. Most likely, he has never had someone accept an invitation the way you did. If he makes a move to kiss you or become more intimate, even to wanting to holding hands, you can gently and apologetically remind him about your need to not be in a relationship right now. As a woman, you can finesse your response to imply that he is desirable and you might like to kiss him, but you must restrain yourself for now.

Warning: Traditionally, "Let's be friends" is a gentle break-up line. Be careful that he does not think you are dumping him. In this situation, he should be encouraged that you want to become better friends and do more activities in the future. Your unique approach might need some discussion.

Toad Detector

The moment of truth has arrived when you can learn a critical piece of information about your date. How does he react? If he keeps pushing you and acts like he will not be satisfied unless there is some physical intimacy, you just learned enough to know this should be your last date. He is telling you that his top priority is your body not your personality. He is ignoring your wishes and focusing on himself and his immediate selfish impulses—two damaging characteristics for a faithful, sensitive husband and father.

All guys will have the same impulses. Initiating an advance is not necessarily the problem. The big red flag starts flapping violently in the air if he persists after you make your wishes absolutely clear.

But I Really Want to Kiss this Guy

Yes, I understand that you may want to kiss him at least as much as he wants to kiss you. Your kiss and physical affections are much better saved for a true relationship. For now, they are perhaps the most efficient tool to discern the true character of the guy. A man's reaction to this situation will reveal his true character early in your acquaintance. If you were to use standard dating procedures, he will get what he wants and expects. He will be quite content and it may take you a long time to know his true character. If you kiss the guy while you intend to stay at the friendship level, you are sending a confusing double message that is unfair to the guy.

Remember, your purpose is to find a great, lifetime, princely husband. You don't have the time or emotional stamina to be in relationships that are going nowhere. The sooner you can discern a guy's toadishness, the less time wasted. Your time is precious. There are a lot more toads than princes, and they will happily divert you for a while if they can. Spare your heart a lot of scars and stay focused.

Men of character can deal with boundaries.

Chapter 20

Creative Dating—Beyond "Get a Video and Hang Out"

YOU LEARN VERY little information about someone by watching a movie together. Sure you will make a few remarks while you watch and perhaps it will get a five-minute review, but movie watching is essentially a passive activity. Movie theaters are the worst because you sit in the dark without uttering a word for two hours. Even for very comfortable friends, it can be awkward to get conversation going after that much dead silence. If you are just getting to know each other, the after-the-silence conversation can be even more challenging.

A better plan is to do activities together. Activities are not romantic, but then, you do not need nor want romance too early. Build a friendship first and see if you enjoy being together as friends. Here are some activity suggestions:

1. Bake cookies together
2. Make a gourmet meal together (Much better than one person doing all the work to impress the other.)
3. Go for a hike (in the woods)
4. Go for a walk (in town)
5. Learn Ballroom dancing, swing dancing, etc.
6. Take turns teaching each other something you are good at. For example, you may be good at knitting, cooking, making

a webpage, and origami. He may be good at carpentry, flower arranging, tennis, scrapbooking, throwing a football, and changing car oil. Teach each other these skills and you've both advanced.

7. Play catch with a baseball, football, or Frisbee.
8. Play Frisbee golf (Use an official course or trees in a park.)
9. Go canoeing or kayaking
10. Have a picnic
11. Fly kites
12. Volunteer together
13. Attend a club or association meeting
14. Waterski
15. Landscape together in one of your yards or for an elderly person
16. Visit a nursing home (This one might be challenging but also revealing.)
17. Make a video together
18. Go rock climbing
19. Visit the library and each pick five interesting books to peruse together
20. Go fishing, mountain biking, or roller blading
21. Go bicycling—short rides or long rides
22. Visit a cemetery and read epitaphs, maybe at night with a flashlight if it is safe and legal
23. Go to the zoo
24. Go to a minor league baseball game (semi-passive)
25. Go to an opera (semi-passive; however, it could generate discussion)
26. Go to church. Visit different denominations together. (Warning—people will assume you are a couple or married.)
27. Play pool or ping pong
28. Learn to surf
29. Visit each other's workplace
30. Train together and run a fundraiser 5K
31. Work the phones for PBS or a charity fundraiser

32. Organize a drawer or a closet or a garage together (definitely not romantic)
33. Paint something
34. Write letters to each other once a week
35. Plan discussion questions like a fake Leno interview
36. Play games together like Scrabble, cards, poker, Monopoly, or checkers
37. Get friends together for a game night or dinner
38. Play Wiffleball, croquet (regular or wacky), or paint ball
39. Go target or skeet shooting
40. Wash the car
41. Visit a tourist attraction
42. Go birdwatching
43. Choose a book club, read the book, and attend the discussions together
44. Choose a book on your own and discuss it with just the two of you. Take turns asking questions.
45. Do an art project together
46. Go hunting together
47. Go to an art museum and discuss what you like or dislike in the art
48. Participate in archery
49. Play Settlers of Cataan (a complex board game)
50. Play musical instruments together
51. Sing together—even with marginal talent
52. Shoot baskets together—maybe make him shoot left handed
53. Do Karaoke—in private or public
54. Go shopping together
55. Participate on an environmental clean-up team
56. Work on a political campaign
57. Go skiing—cross country or downhill (Chairlift rides are great for short conversations.)
58. Take a wildflower walk
59. Play miniature golf
60. Work with kids

You may be geek, goth, athlete, intellectual, active, or sedentary. You may either be an outdoorsman or an indoor person, but even if some of these suggestions made you gag, you should find a few ideas that could work for you. Are you willing to try new things? The beauty of activities is that the activity itself becomes a topic of conversation, so you do not need to work as hard thinking of something interesting to talk about.

Learn a Lot in a Little Time

Many of these activities allow you to see how the guy interacts with others. Is he polite? Does he converse with others? Do others like and respect him? Of all the people you are around in the activity, is his personality the most appealing to you? Does he embarrass you in a crowd or make you proud to be with him? Is he a gentleman? Does he protect and take care of you? Does he get angry when things go wrong? Does he tease you if you are not good at something? Is he more concerned about you having a good time or him having a good time? How does he interact with children?

You could watch a hundred movies together and not learn as much as you would from a single canoe outing. Think outside the video box.

Note: Many guys do not think with this much creativity, but they would probably be very receptive to these ideas. Guys often do not want to take a risk inviting you to do something unusual, so they go for the standard, safe, but often awkward movie date.

Accept or Modify

When you are asked out to a movie, one option is to accept the invitation "as is," make the best of it, and bring up other more creative possibilities if you think a second date is likely. You can also turn down the invitation and make an alternative suggestion. You could say something like, "Thank you so much for inviting me to a movie. I'm sorry I have plans for that night (remember, your plans could be to give yourself a manicure, but it is still a plan and works perfectly fine as an on-the-spot escape route.) I would love to do something with you another time. I've always wanted to explore the nature trail that is near the park. Would you like to do something like that sometime?" Then if he accepts, maybe you could play catch or Frisbee golf or play on the swings while at the park. Making suggestions might be a bit forward but it shifts you into an activity that will be much more comfortable for both of you than a movie. Be careful, though, that you do not get in the habit of always having a "better" idea than his.

Hopefully, when you have the freedom, security, and encouragement to date creatively, he will initiate creative dates as well. If he needs help, hand him this list and tell him it is multiple choice—pick one.

Chapter 21

How to Dump a Guy Humanely

VARIOUS OCCASIONS WILL inevitably arise for every woman in which she must turn down a guy.

Three examples

1. A guy asks you out and you would not go if he were the last living male on earth.
2. You have been out once or twice with a guy. He invites you again but you have decided you do not want to continue the relationship.
3. He invites you and you want to go, but you honestly have a conflict.

If you do not consider situations such as these ahead of time, when they occur, you will probably experience a wave of panic as you scramble to make up some kind of scheduling excuse. The moment will be awkward for both of you. You may find yourself taking evasive maneuvers to try to avoid the guy when you think an invitation might be brewing. Some girls become purposely rude to prevent the invitation. Such situations are not necessary if you develop a foolproof plan ahead of time. You can relax and be your normal friendly self.

Knowing how to turn down a guy gracefully is especially important if you follow through with becoming an expert at conversation. Men will find you friendly, interesting, and especially easy to talk to. Men normally have so much difficulty with conversation that they feel a sense of security when the conversation is flowing easily. Your skills with conversation will bring more invitations your way, but some of them you obviously will not want to accept.

Men are less complicated than women when it comes to relationships. Men like to know where they stand. If you are excited about them, they want to know. If they have absolutely no chance with you, they want to know that too. A rejection might be initially painful to hear, but men really do want to know the truth. Lots of other girls are out there. Guys usually get over the pain quickly and move on. Before asking you, your date probably spent some time daydreaming about you as the perfect girlfriend or wife—creating some inaccurate vision of you and him together. Until he asks you out, that fantasy continues to grow in his head. You are appealing to him because in his dream, you are crazy about him. Once he asks you and finds out you really have no interest, his dream will lose that important element and will fade away. If he is in limbo, the dream remains. Do him a favor and don't leave him in limbo land. He will take it like a man especially if it's early in the relationship.

Declining an invitation is difficult for many of you because you are naturally compassionate. Even if you don't like the guy, you don't want to hurt him. However, if you understand the male mind, you will know that the best thing for both of you is for you to be completely honest with him. Do not actually tell him that you would not go out with him if he were the last breathing man on earth. You can be honest and firm, yet kind and tactful all at the same time.

A good supervisor in the workplace knows a very useful technique for breaking bad news to an employee, and it works equally well with bad news for the guy with whom you are dealing.

Here is the magic formula …

Step 1—Thanks

Thank the man for something. You can always find something for which to be thankful. In the workplace, the supervisor might say, "Jones, thank you for the hard work you put in on the last project." Applied to the dating world, your thankful phrase would be something like this, "Herman, thank you for thinking of me. I am honored."

Step 2—Delay or Dump

For step two you have two options, the delay tactic or the hit-him-between-the-eyes move.

Delay

For the delay option, you simply say something like, "I will need to check my schedule. Can I get back to you?" or "I will need to check with my parents. Can I get back to you?" Do not give any more information or possible excuses. Such phrases often sound like excuses and can get you trapped if you say too much. The bonus is that this technique works with almost all invitations. It seems obvious, but I was well into adulthood before I stopped fishing for lame excuses and just dropped one of these helpful lines. The schedule delay is the truth because checking this date definitely will prevent you from double booking yourself. The parent delay is the truth if you are a teen living at home. Best of all, these delays give you time to think.

The guy might be in the grey area of acceptability and you want to think or even pray about what you should do next. If this is the case, asking a few questions is another delay technique that will help you evaluate his offer. Ask when, where, who, what, why, and how concerning the outing. His answers might be the influencers of your decision and you can make a more informed choice.

Or

Dump Gently

Even though you're dumping the guy, do so gently. Always hit him with a positive comment before any negatives. An employer has time to think about this ahead of time and come up with something positive to say. Even the worst employee has done something positive. "Jones,

I noticed you threw away a paper cup in the lunch room last week. I appreciate that." In the dating scenario, finding a sincere compliment can be tough if the invitation is totally unexpected. Also you might be anxious to get to the point. A thousand reasons why you would never go out with him pop into your mind, but you must suppress these for this conversation. You need not shoot these poisonous darts with him. Instead, graciously say something encouraging to him such as, "Herman, I think you are a nice guy" or "Herman, I enjoyed having you in our study group" or "Herman, I enjoy working with you." Some of these might be stretching the truth if the guy is a total toad, but usually the man has had some rapport with you that influenced him to ask you out in the first place. Many girls are reluctant to say anything at all positive because they are afraid it will encourage him. No worries. Step three will remedy any false hopes he may have.

Step 3—But …

The third step—After the thanks and your positive statement, you add a "but." The whole line could sound something like this, "Herman, thank you for thinking of me. I'm honored. You're a nice guy, but I don't think it would be a good idea for us to go out together. Well, I need to go. See you later."

Now this moment is the most difficult because you just popped his bubble. Some guys will ask out just about anybody they see. For them, this rejection might be no more traumatic than finding out the video they wanted to rent is unavailable. For other guys though, they might have been planning the question for a month. Either way, if you are certain you do not want to go out with him, you must hang tough at this moment.

Most guys will understand that they have just been flatly rejected and will let it go. Some guys, however, are slow learners or believe persistence might win you over. Here is a great way to deal with the persistent guy.

Broken Record Technique

I learned this great technique in *Conversationally Speaking*. It works for any situation in which someone is trying to get you to do something you do not want to do. Essentially, you acknowledge the legitimacy of any arguments or reasoning tossed your way, then you repeat your position.

> Here's how it might pan out after you completed step three.
> Guy: "But it is a really good movie. I know you will like it."
> You: "Yes, it probably is a good movie, but I would prefer not to go."
> Guy: "I heard you tell Jen that you wanted to see it."
> You: "Yes, I did talk to Jen about it, but I would prefer not to go."
> Guy: "Why don't you want to go?"
> You: "I would just prefer not to go."

If he has not figured out by now that he has been denied, you are dealing with a serious toad. Regardless of his persistence or emotion, you owe him no further explanation. You are fully entitled to your opinion and you have no obligation to go into detail just because he asks you for details. At this point he is being too dense to understand that you are graciously sparing him from the gory details of why you really will not go out with him.

This technique works because you have completely disarmed him calmly with a smile. No squirming or hesitation. You can be gentle and understanding of his disappointment and embarrassment but unyielding in your response. The big bonus here is that you can disarm the world's best salesmen with this technique too. In order for a salesman to get you to buy, he must learn the reasons you do not want to buy and then overcome those objections. If you do not give him any reasons, he has no idea what to say to win you over. As soon as you reveal one of your objections, the salesman or your male suitor will introduce a new line of reasoning into the conversation for you to counter. The next time you find yourself face-to-face with a salesman of any sort, remember this valuable escape route.

I suggest you reread these last few paragraphs and visualize yourself and what you would say. Go through the entire scenario in your head so you have rehearsed your response. You want to be like a finely trained pilot—prepared to react instinctively to any emergency.

Telling a man the truth is much more humane than dragging him along because you do not have the courage to do so. A common response to an unwanted invitation is to tell the guy you are busy that night. Sorry, that's not fair, particularly if it's not true. Simply saying you are busy can leave him wondering whether you really are busy or just looking for an excuse. If he asks a second time and gets the same response, he may figure it out, but it might even take a third call. Each of these follow-up calls take an extra measure of courage since he anticipates that rejection is likely. Why put him through all that just because you do not have the backbone to tell him the truth? He has paid you the highest compliment in saying that he would like to spend time with you. You owe him the courtesy of an honest response.

If you have been out a few times and want to break it off, follow the same three-step process. Thank him for the dates, tell him something you enjoyed about him, and then tell him that you want to keep things as "just friends."

If you are asked out by someone you like, but you genuinely have a conflict, be sure to tell him that you would love to go out with him and you hope he will ask again. Otherwise, the "I am busy" response is often interpreted as a subtle rejection. Without your encouraging response, he might not call again. For a man, the second call after an initial rejection is very difficult to make. If you want another call, be sure to tell him so. He will be floating instead of sitting in uncomfortable limbo land.

In the Creative Dating chapter, I talked about what to do if you like the guy but not the plan for the date.

Chapter 22

Never Say I Love You

"I LOVE …" IS a phrase tossed around lightly by society. I love that song. I love dark chocolate. I love a back rub. I love Aunt Maude. These phrases are all harmless misuses of the word love. Unfortunately, most of us use "I love you" in an intimate relationship without thinking about what we are saying. It seems that once we start to get in deep with someone, that phrase starts to pop up. It gives the relationship a more serious sense of commitment.

How wonderful it is to have that phrase aimed at us. We all want to be loved by someone. The problem is that this most powerful phrase in the world is cheapened if we say it when we don't really mean it. We commonly whisper those magic words in special intimate moments before or after a kiss. It doesn't sound right to say, "Good night, I really, really like you." So to sound smooth and build the relationship we whisper "I love you."

Although some people say it just because it's expected or to manipulate the other person, many people truly believe it when they say and hear it. The problem is with their understanding of what love means. A common description would be a powerful feeling or attraction to someone. True love may start as a powerful feeling, but it requires a decision and commitment to love another person. True love means you are committed to the other person even when you don't feel like it.

The problem becomes obvious when the relationship begins to cool down, and we lose the fuzzy feelings. We may fall out of love and stop saying "I love you." Our "love" evaporates until we get in our next relationship. Yo-yoing in and out of "love" is an unhealthy practice that teaches the erroneous concept that true love can blossom and then dry up. Your marriage will be at risk if you believe your love can die. Love that lasts a lifetime must be fed daily with commitment and sacrifice. We need to remember that our feelings will ebb and flow, but the love we have for our mate must be a permanent decision that is not controlled by our feelings. Every day, we must decide to love our spouse.

True love means you are committed to the other person even when you don't feel like it.

I did not tell Ruth I loved her until the day I proposed. She was confused because she thought we were very serious, and she expected me to say the three words earlier in the relationship. However, I had not filled her in on that eclectic part of my dating philosophy. As a woman, you should be aware that the chances are good that the man whispering "I love you" in your ear has no idea what he is talking about. You may think he is in love with you and contemplating a lifetime commitment or marriage. He may be thinking, *This is what I am supposed to say at this point in the relationship* or *If I tell her I love her, she is more likely to sleep with me.* Same words—radically different meanings. Just something to think about the next time you speak or hear that phrase.

Never say I love you … until you mean it for a lifetime.

Section Three

DON'T SLEEP WITH HIM

Why Not

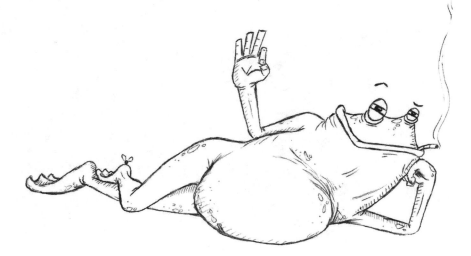

Chapter 23

Baffled by Instinct

HAVE YOU EVER watched a hunting dog point to a bird? One front leg is lifted, the tail is straight back and the body is absolutely motionless. No one trained the dog to do this. As it grows, it points automatically because of the instinct. Birds with brains the size of peas navigate flawlessly on their annual migration. The rare Horny Headed East Mongolian Blue Bodied Beetle somehow finds another beetle under a log in the forest with which it can make baby beetles. Instinct is obvious in creatures around us every day. People, on the other hand, did not seem to get many instincts apart from maybe hunger and channel surfing. Of our few instincts, sexual attraction is powerful enough to shape much of our lives. We do not have to be taught or encouraged to be attracted to the opposite sex; that happens all by itself.

Humans have great intelligence and self awareness, yet, bizarrely, we can be totally tripped up by this incredible force of nature. Unlike the animal kingdom, humans have the intelligence and potential for self control that can cause us to refrain from taking action on our instinctive thoughts and impulses. By contrast, the only force keeping the male musk ox from breeding with all the females in the herd is a bigger musk ox. Even the most self-aware musk ox has no moral or practical reason not to breed with any female that might be available.

The Swan

You may already know that swans mate for life. Many people find this natural monogamy to be cute and romantic in waterfowl. We humans have the same monogamous instinct but we often choose to violate it. Any person having sex with someone other than his/her spouse has an instinctive sense of guilt because a natural law is being broken. We might feel guilty because we know our parents would disapprove, but even if no one ever suggested that having sex outside of marriage is wrong, we already know it. We may learn to ignore the guilt, but deep down, we know we are wired for monogamy just like the swan.

Humans, with our great intellect, have many moral, spiritual, and practical reasons not to mate with each other indiscriminately. Most people would agree with me so far. Since I believe I have very little chance of changing your moral or spiritual convictions in this short book, I would like to make the attempt to convince you with practical reasons that sex outside of marriage is a bad idea if you hope to eventually enjoy a lifelong, steady diet of passionate intimate sex with your spouse. I would like to convince you logically and practically that having sex before you are married will drastically reduce your odds of finding and keeping the passion in your future marriage. I understand completely that this contradicts the accepted dating and mating philosophy of our society.

Chapter 24

Recipe for Success

LIFE IS LIKE A BATCH OF COOKIES

IF YOU HAD the world's greatest recipe for chocolate chip cookies, you could make an incredible batch if you carefully follow the recipe from start to finish. Unfortunately, one simple mistake, like substituting a cup of salt instead of a cup of sugar, would ruin the entire batch.

Relationships are a thousand times more complex than cookies and it is impossible to predict if you will have a great marriage. But, there are many dating mistakes that can harm your relationship and future marriage just as predictably as a cup of salt in your cookie dough. One of the biggest mistakes is also one of the most common mistakes—sleeping with the man before you are married. Most people would consider sex to be the cup of sugar in the cookie dough analogy, but it turns out to be much more like a cup of salt.

If life is a batch of cookie dough, remember you only get one batch. Once you dump in the salt, you may be dealing with that salt for the rest of your life. Some baking mishaps are still edible but not nearly as pleasurable. You will survive your relational mishaps, but your life may be less pleasant. What is your recipe for finding the love of your life?

Chapter 25

Who Are You?

WOMEN COULD BE divided into three general categories in their views of sex. Which one best describes you?

Sex Is for Marriage

You believe that sex is for marriage and your preference or commitment would be that your first sexual experience is with your husband after you are married. Perhaps you have a spiritual, moral, or rational foundation that has led to this belief.

If that describes you, I hope I can pile on enough support to help you stick with your convictions while the rest of the world, your emotions, and physical desires conspire to push you to change your mind.

Sex Is Acceptable for Mature Adults in a Committed Relationship

Most people in the United States would probably fall into this category. You are a reasonable and likeable person who has thought it through and who sees nothing wrong with sex between mature, committed, consenting adults. You would not sleep with a guy unless it was in the context of a committed relationship. Sex is a normal part of a good relationship. You enjoy it as much as the guy and see no reason not to do it. You believe that in this age, it is unreasonable to expect mature adults to refrain. After all, your reasoning is that having sex now is the best way to confirm that you will be completely compatible before you get married.

If you fit this description, you are my primary audience because you are already thinking logically and are receptive to logical arguments. I hope you will read carefully with an open mind to determine if my logic holds up. I make many dire predictions of what can be expected if the laws of love and sex are ignored. If I am wrong, you have nothing to worry about.

Casual Sex Is Fine

If you are in this category, you are willing to have sexual encounters with men you recently met or barely know. These encounters are exciting and make you feel wanted; you see nothing wrong with them. Many others are doing the same thing. Eventually, you hope to meet a guy who will be "the one." Also included in this category are "friends with benefits." These are friends who have sex with each other with no strings attached—just for the fun of it.

If this description sounds like you, I expect you have already experienced some of the painful heartache that I suggest is inherent in superficial sexual relationships. Hopefully, some of my reasoning will make sense to you. I realize it would be a radical lifestyle change if you were to adopt some of the suggestions in this book. I strongly believe and will try to prove that the change will be well worth it.

Chapter 26

You Can't Put a Condom on Your Heart

THE MOST COMMON reasons I hear for people to abstain from sex unless they are married are: to avoid pregnancy, to avoid sexually transmitted diseases, and because it is wrong. God says it is wrong.

These reasons all may seem legitimate; however, the first two reasons can generally be resolved by birth control or condoms, although not as reliably as you may think. The last reason only counts if you care what God thinks. If you are not religious, you have no moral reason to deny yourself the pleasure you could enjoy through sex. In fact, if you have no moral reason to keep sex only in marriage, you would be crazy to deny yourself the ultimate pleasure. That is unless there are other reasons to avoid single sex. Sex without marriage is so completely accepted by our society that it seems absurd that any normal person would expect to have another standard. It may seem totally unrealistic in today's "enlightened" society.

What if there are some other rational, pragmatic reasons not to have sex while you are single? I believe participating in premarital sex is probably the biggest obstacle that may keep you from finding your love of a lifetime and leave you confused and diverted down roads that will not take you where you want to go. Sex, by its very nature, is guaranteed to increase your pleasure temporarily, and I believe it will be just as reliable in increasing your pain level for the long term. I know abstinence is a radical concept today, but I hope you will read on and determine if you agree with me by the end. Your heart and your love depend on your critical decision in this area. You can use a condom to protect yourself from unwanted pregnancy and many STDs, but you cannot put a condom on your heart. Nothing protects your heart from the emotional scars of sexual experiences that fall apart and leave a woman shattered. If you are sexually active, I hope this statement burns deeply into your memory to reappear the next time a condom is about to be used. Next time, administer the Love Test instead, so you can know where you really stand in the relationship. Read the Foolproof Toad Detector chapter.

By the way, condoms do not stop the Human papillomavirus which is rampant today and causes genital warts as well as increasing the risk of cervical cancers. "Safe sex" with a condom is misleading. Condoms reduce the risk but do not eliminate it.

Chapter 27

Sex Is like Duct Tape

THE CREDIT FOR this sticky analogy goes to University of Texas professor J. Budziszewski who was the first to recognize that sex is like duct tape. The first time you use duct tape, it creates a bond to whatever it touches. However, the more you rip it off and try to re-stick it, the less sticky it becomes. It's the same with sex. The first time you have sex with someone, you create a bond with him. However, the more you rip away and have sex with others, the less "sticky" or bonded you become. Budziszewski writes, "You just don't stick anymore, your sexual partners seem like strangers, and you stop feeling." Previous partners can result in diminished pleasure in sex in the long term (marriage). Not a good trade off.

Let me lay out this eloquent analogy a little further.

1. Duct tape is strong. Sex creates a strong bond that helps married couples stick together.
2. Duct tape sticks the best the first time it is used. Sex is most powerful when used on one and only one relationship. A powerful bond occurs during sex (particularly for the woman).
3. Duct tape loses stickiness each time it is reused. Each time sex is experienced with a new partner, the magic and the bonding power is diminished until it has very little effect at all. It could still be pleasurable, but the miraculous bonding power can be virtually destroyed (like used duct tape).

4. Duct tape hurts when removed from skin. When a relationship is broken, the pain is greater for the woman if sex was part of the relationship. Just as the tape can rip hairs from your arm, sex can rip out a piece of your heart.

Sexually speaking, each person gets just one piece of duct tape. Your best use of that tape would be to apply it very deliberately for the full adhesion effect with your husband of a lifetime. You will share the pinnacle of human pleasure and oneness together. Sex binds couples together in a way that cannot be expressed with words.

If you waste your precious strip of duct tape on someone other than your husband, you will not only experience the pain of the tape removal, but you will also diminish the bonding effect with whoever ends up being your husband. No matter how hard you try, you will have memories and comparisons locked in your mind. This memory chip cannot be erased. Use your duct tape wisely.

When sex is used just for fun such as casual hookups or "friends with benefits," it loses its mystique and part of its bonding power so important for marriage. Why dilute one of the most important ingredients of your future marriage?

Important Note: If you have already mangled your duct tape, do not despair. There is hope. In fact, there is an amazing remedy. It is beyond the scope of this book but you can learn more about the remedy at FindingYourPrince.com

Note: J. Budziszewski has many other interesting viewpoints in his book, **Ask Me Anything**.

Comments from **Hurt: Inside the World of Today's Teenagers (Youth, Family, and Culture)** by Chap Clark. *I was surprised to realize that for most mid-adolescents, the issue of sex has lost its mystique and has become almost commonplace. They have been conditioned to expect so much from sex and have been so tainted by overexposure and the emptiness of valueless banter and play that they have become jaded and laisse-faire in their attitudes. As one student told me, "Sex is a game and a toy, nothing more." As I was to find out, it is also more than that—it is a temporary salve for the pain and loneliness resulting from abandonment.*

Chapter 28

Intended for Pleasure— Why Sex Was Invented

"The first bond of society is marriage."

—Cicero

How in the World Sex Works

1. Sex is needed to have babies and keep the species going.
2. Babies turn into children. Children seem to do best when they grow up in strong, happy, healthy families with a mom and dad who love each other.
3. Society does best when it has more happy families than dysfunctional, unhappy families.
4. Troubled children from dysfunctional, unhappy families are more likely to break things, steal, scare people, rape women, and generally contribute to making other people less happy. Therefore, strong, happy, complete families are the essential foundation to a civilized society. What does it take to make happy and healthy families? One of the critical ingredients is sex.

"They say it takes a village to raise a child. That may be the case, but the truth is that it takes a lot of solid, stable marriages to create a village."

—Diane Sollee

Why We Need Sex

PEOPLE ARE PATHETIC, myself included. Take an honest look at what you do and think when no one is looking and you will be reminded of how imperfect we are. When two imperfect people live together—married or not—they have problems. (Read the Gutterslime chapter). All couples have problems, but some become strong and happy while others become dysfunctional and unhappy.

What would it take to keep imperfect couples together and keep them generally in the happy category more than in the unhappy category? Marriage.

Marriage comes with a lifetime commitment and two of the most powerful forces in the universe, love and sex. Keeping two imperfect people together and happy for a lifetime is one of the toughest challenges we face, so it calls for two of the most powerful tools. Love brings many wonderful things into the relationship like kindness, self-sacrifice, patience, humility, trust, forgiveness, and peacefulness, all noble ideas and skills that can be learned and developed.

However, people are not always responsive to noble ideas, so something physical was needed as part of the magic equation of marriage; and thus, sex was invented. Men and women were given an insatiable physical craving for one another. We always come back for more. We don't need to be taught to be attracted to each other; it just happens and it is powerful. Both the higher ideals of love and the physical power of sex are needed to maximize number two and minimize number four from the list above so the world is a suitable place to live.

The Power of Sex

In an already strong relationship, sex draws the couple together and makes almost everything better. It motivates couples to overlook flaws, speeds forgiveness, inspires romance, builds spiritual and emotional unity, smoothes out the bumps of life, and provides a lifetime reason for a husband and wife to be nice to each other—they hope to have sex soon.

Magnetized

A married couple is like two magnets that are held close together. They have a magnetic attraction that makes the magnets want to come together and become one. Even when they are not together, an electromagnetic field exists between them. For a husband and wife, a positive sexual tension lingers between the satisfaction of their last time together and the anticipation of their next time. Sounds rather sensual? It *is* sensual during the best of times. When the relationship is healthy, the marriage can cruise in this zone much of the time and life is good. Unfortunately, sick kids, exhaustion, job stress, and the rest of life force our attention elsewhere. Even the best marriages have arguments and anger. How couples respond to the anger reveals the true quality of the relationship. One thing is for certain, anger and sex do not mix. A healthy marriage can enjoy the magnetic attraction through all seasons of life only if both people are continually working at keeping the underlying love alive. It requires deliberate commitment and sacrifice to put the other person first.

None of this electrically-charged sexual atmosphere happens if the underlying relationship is unstable or cracking. In an unhealthy relationship, sex becomes a wedge that pushes couples even further apart. If the two magnets are moved far enough apart, no attractive force is felt. If the magnets get turned around, they can even repel each other. Interestingly, the repellent force of sex is just as powerful as its attractive force. Repellent forces go to work in weak relationships. Sex will not smooth over a major argument or a significant rift in the relationship. In those situations, it can create an ugly array of resentment, confusion, coercion, depression, humiliation, exploitation, and anger.

So sex makes a good marriage great and a poor marriage terrible. If you get married without all the building blocks needed for a solid relationship, you are setting yourself up for lots of pain when the thrill of your physical relationship starts to wear thin. Many people have confused the thrill of a sexual relationship with the thrill of being truly in love. By the time they realize their mistake, they already have children whom they love more than they love each other. The kids then grow up in a hostile home or become victims of divorce.

A Fairy Tale

In some ways the mysterious power is like a fairy tale in which a wizard has created a love potion called sex. It is a magic potion that can make all your dreams come true, but there is one important thing you must always remember. If used improperly, your dream can transform into a nightmare! A puff of smoke and the wizard disappears with a frightening ironic laugh.

The trouble for singles is that they feel all the same forces of attraction that are needed for marriage, but they are not married. When singles try to use the "potion" improperly (outside of marriage), their problems have just begun.

Note: When you are ready to marry Mr. Right, read the book by Dr. Ed Wheat, *Intended for Pleasure*. It is an excellent, thorough how-to guide for sex. Husband and wife should read it before the honeymoon.

"When there is love in a marriage,
there is harmony in the home;
when there is harmony in the home,
there is contentment in the community;
when there is contentment in the community,
there is prosperity in the nation;
when there is prosperity in the nation,
there is peace in the world."

—Chinese proverb

Chapter 29

A Pretend Marriage

Living Together Makes Sense at First

RATIONAL PEOPLE MIGHT use this as the justification for living together or sleeping together. You could argue that it would be unwise to make a lifetime commitment to someone without testing the durability of the relationship. "So let's live as though we are married and see how it goes," seems like good, cautious judgment on the surface. In reality, it is the highest risk option you can choose. Why? Because you underestimate the power of sex.

Sex is so powerful, it can keep a relationship rolling along for years. This honeymoon phase can last a week or years. During this time you are as intimate as a married couple but without any commitment. Both of you are in your prime (you are not getting younger). You are out of the dating pool. If you are not with your prince and your prince is looking for you, he will not find you. If you became sexually active early in the relationship, the rest of your relationship is growing in slow motion because he, like all men, would rather have sex than talk. You have used the powerful glue intended for true marriage to glue your trial marriage together. Sex is strong, but not strong enough to overcome all of the petty imperfections of a couple. It holds you together as long as it can, But as the relationship starts to crumble, sex mysteriously loses its effect. In fact, it does a 180-degree turn and becomes a wedge between you.

By now, you have been out of the dating routine for awhile. You have aged and been rejected. You are horrified by the thought of loneliness. Your options are to stay in the terrible relationship or face the loneliness in your slightly damaged condition. You may be less desirable to the prince you desired in the first place.

Scott Stanley, a University of Denver psychologist, has spent the last 15 years studying why premarital cohabitation is associated with lower levels of satisfaction in marriage and greater potential for divorce. Studies have shown that men who cohabitated before marriage were, on average, less dedicated to their relationships than those who didn't. He also describes a phenomenon that he calls sliding vs. deciding in which couples commonly avoid making decisions about their relationship and just glide along ambiguously. Sliding can happen at any stage of a relationship but it becomes especially problematic if you slide into cohabitation. He found that many people tend to stay in non-committed relationships longer than they should and sometimes slide into children and marriage without ever really making a decision. Learn more about his cohabitation and relationship studies at http://slidingvsdeciding. blogspot.com/

Only one in ten couples who live together are together after five years. Your "cautious, rational" plan has a 90% chance of failure with some serious consequences if it does fail. The 10% who might get married, still have a 50% chance of divorce. Those are not good odds. If you felt desperate before, wait until you emerge at the other end of this dark tunnel after wasting all that time living with someone for nothing.

Both men and women live longer, happier, healthier,
and wealthier lives when they are married.
Unmarried co-habitation doesn't cut it.
Cohabitation does not bring the benefits—in physical health,
wealth, and emotional well-being—that marriage does.
And, married people have both more and better sex
than do their unmarried counterparts.

—Linda Waite, *The Case for Marriage*

Chapter 30

Try Before You Buy

ANOTHER COMMON RATIONALE for sleeping together before a couple gets married is to be sure that they are sexually compatible, i.e. they want to "try before you buy." On the surface, this makes a lot of sense. It is driven by the premise that a woman might marry a man whom she thinks she knows, then on her wedding night, she finds out that he is sexually dangerous or unpleasant. I agree this situation is frightening and I am sure it has happened many times. However, if a couple has built a solid, intimate relationship from a foundation of genuine friendship; if they have avoided the physical intimacy that masquerades as true intimacy; if they have sought good premarital counseling that has guided them into genuine discussions about the serious issues of life; if they are spiritually compatible; and if her friends and family saw no clues that a monster is lurking inside, then rest assured, they will be sexually compatible. The conscious decision to sleep with your boyfriend is a significant fork in the road of life. We have much safer and more effective ways to evaluate the potential for long term compatibility than sleeping together.

Artificial Intimacy

When you sleep together before marriage, you risk much but learn very little that will help to evaluate your relationship. Sex, by its very nature will produce intense feelings; however, the *physical* intimacy can create a false *emotional* intimacy. Artificial intimacy becomes especially confusing for the woman because she craves emotional intimacy and she feels intense emotional intimacy, but it is not really there. For a man to be physically intimate with little or no emotional intimacy is very easy. The woman assumes emotional intimacy is there, but it likely is not. If the sexual experience revealed that the guy was unpleasant or dangerous in bed, I contend that if you had spent more time getting to know the guy, you could have discovered that tendency without sleeping with him and hurting yourself. Without a doubt, a woman is injured one way or another by sleeping with a monster. The damage you can cause to yourself is much greater than any benefit you hope to find. Having sex to evaluate a relationship is not wise or logical.

Commitment
"It is not your love that sustains the marriage, but from now on, the marriage that sustains your love."

—Dietrich Bonhoeffer,
*writing to a young bride and groom from his
prison cell in Nazi Germany in 1943*

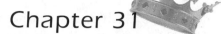

Chapter 31

Men Are Microwaves, Women Are Crockpots

THE KITCHEN APPLIANCE example that says "men are microwaves and women are crockpots" is a helpful analogy of the fundamental difference between men and women in the area of sexuality. Men are very quick in their transition from non-sexual to sexual thoughts and action. Men are also very quick in the gratification/ejaculation department. Overall, men are built for speed—just like a microwave, but, as you know, a microwave is not an instrument of culinary nuances, and men are often not very subtle when it comes to sex. Fortunately, men can learn to be slow, subtle, and nuanced. Men's quick transition from non-sexual to sexual thoughts is important to know because your safety can change very quickly if you are with a persuasive or aggressive guy who suddenly experiences sexual urges.

Women, on the other hand, tend to be much slower in their sexual response—like a crockpot. The pot might be plugged in and turned on but it takes a while to heat up. In fact, no heat may be detected for awhile; however, eventually it will become too hot to touch and will get the food cooked. It all takes time. It also takes a while to cool down.

Great Lovers Are Made, Not Born

Another piece of sex advice Ruth and I share during our premarital counseling is this little truism, "If the man does what comes naturally, he will be doing almost everything wrong when it comes to maximizing his wife's pleasure" because naturally, men are focused on themselves. Men are built for quick and easy gratification. The starting point of the natural sexual state of a man is pretty close to a rabbit. If you have ever seen rabbits mate, or most animals for that matter, "the act" happens in a flash. If you blink, you might miss it. As a veterinarian, I have seen lots of animals mate. I remember thinking many times, "That's it? It happened so fast, will we really get a baby lamb out of that in the spring?" Well, guess what? Spring comes and there's the lamb! Sheep and rabbits are fine with that quick process, but in a marriage, that's not so good.

Built for Speed but He's Not Superman

Contrast the man's natural speed with the woman's slow crockpot pace and you see that something has got to give. Biologically, the woman is basically stuck with her crockpottedness; therefore, the husband must make most of the adjustments and learn how to please his slow-heating wife. Through premarital counseling and reading, a man can know and understand the female anatomy, physiology, and psychology.

Brilliant men from all of human history haven't understood the female mind. I doubt that your boyfriend has new revelations of wisdom. Even when he knows the basics of what he is supposed to do, he probably will be unable to do it skillfully initially. A man needs lots of practice to become a good lover. If he has gained experience by having sex with other women, his sexual resume should be a serious red flag.

Once a couple knows the basics, they spend the rest of the marriage teaching each other what they personally enjoy. Only the dumbest husband in the world will not want to sign up for the class in which his wife wants him in bed to teach him how to please her the most. May your class be in session for as long as you both shall live with each of you acting as teachers. You and your husband will need a lifetime of sex education from each other and a lifetime commitment is the only way to provide the security you need. A couple must have the solid foundation of a permanent relationship in order to know the emotional security that allows complete vulnerability, complete oneness, and a complete marriage. Completeness is part of the dream I described in the first chapter. There is no shortcut to arrive at this point. Allowing yourself to become totally vulnerable with someone who is not totally and permanently committed to your welfare is foolish and dangerous.

Chapter 32

Ghosts in My Bed

Perma-Memory

YOU CAN'T REMEMBER the name of a mountain range in Burma for a geography test or where you left your car keys but there are some memories and experiences you never forget. Yes, you guessed it once again—sex. A special section of the brain is reserved for sexual images and experiences. What goes in stays in whether you want it or not. Thus, you get a memory bank of sexual experiences to keep with you forever; it's automatic. A married man I know describes the feeling as ghosts in his bed from his memories of previous sex partners. He can't shake them.

Good Memories Are Bad

The problem for a couple with previous sex partners is that all those partners climb into bed with you when you are married. Some of them might have been more exciting or prettier than the spouse. The memory that was locked in could be from an exciting encounter. Many relationships are especially exciting at the beginning before you know each other well enough to spot all of the flaws. Every experience is locked in for a lifetime of compare and contrast with your spouse. Your memory of that hunky guy remains as a hunky guy—maybe even hunkier as time goes on. Unfortunately, your hubby may grow large and round in the midsection. Dissatisfaction seeps in. Your husband's memories of his previous sex partners will have the same effect on him. The seeds for divorce are planted. Hopefully, the seeds will not grow, but the risk factor is there.

Bad Memories Are Bad

Memories might be from bad experiences that left you in physical and emotional pain. It could be from molestation or bad choices to have sex. Women learn to create emotional barriers from bad experiences. If every time she opened up and allowed herself to be vulnerable, she got burned by a man, normal survival techniques would have her closing down emotionally to avoid the pain. Just as you blink to prevent something getting in your eye, your emotions can close up to prevent emotional damage. Unfortunately, emotions do not rebound in the blink of an eye; damage can last for years. Closed emotions will not work very well for a lifetime of passion and oneness with your husband.

Healthy, intact vulnerable emotions are an essential part of every female, especially for meaningful sex with her husband. If emotions have been stomped on by previous intimate experiences, the marriage is at greater risk. An emotionally scarred wife is a huge problem for the princely husband because much of his satisfaction comes from satisfying his wife. Without healthy emotions, she might be difficult or impossible to satisfy.

A girl can still obviously have sex with her emotions closed—which is fine for the toad guy since he doesn't understand nor care about her emotions anyway. It's all about him. Not so in a healthy marriage. A prince husband will very much want to satisfy his wife and will struggle if her damaged emotions make her satisfaction elusive.

Chapter 33

Friends with Benefits

FRIENDS WITH BENEFITS describes male and female friends or acquaintances who have sex with no strings attached to the relationship. It is simply an entertaining activity like watching a video together or playing a game. "With benefits" sex is just a meaningless toy that provides temporary relief from loneliness or boredom. No commitment is implied or expected. It's just for fun. It may be meaningless but it is not harmless. Let's compare it to Mona Lisa and see why.

During college I traveled with a backpack for a few weeks through Europe and found myself in the Louvre in Paris—one of the top museums in the world. Many masterpieces are found here but the Mona Lisa painting by Leonardo da Vinci is the best of the best. When you enter the room to view Mona, you see a special section with extra barriers, perfect lighting, and a crowd of people gathered to admire her. I had a sense of awe looking directly at such a famous painting—the real thing. The room is filled with hushed voices as others feel the same sense of wonder and respect. The masterpiece painting in the proper setting creates an amazing experience. This scene represents sex as it can and should be.

Imagine if you took the actual Mona Lisa painting from her place of honor, cut it from the frame, and used it as a placemat. Crushed Cheerios®, spilled grape juice, and splattered spaghetti sauce would quickly transform the painting from a priceless masterpiece to a valueless stained sheet.

In the same way, we can diminish the awe and wonder of sexuality if we do not give it the respect and protection it deserves. When sex is treated casually like an everyday placemat, its value and power are destroyed. "Friends with benefits" may seem like a harmless way to fill a void in your life, but sex is a masterpiece of humanity. If you treat your sexuality like a meaningless toy, that's what it will become. You may lose the magic of sex for your future marriage. It may be just as difficult to repair your trivialized sexuality as it would be to rejuvenate the juice-stained Mona Lisa.

Chapter 34

Sags, Bulges, and Wrinkles
It's All Down Hill from Here

THERE GOES A middle-aged guy with his new young wife and sports car tooling down the road. His first wife, after giving birth to all of his children, is sagging, bulging, wrinkled, and divorced. All women are headed down the road to wrinkles—another reason you should be sure he loves your interior character as much as your glossy exterior. Your body is certain to change. If pregnancy is in your future, stretch marks are too. Will he still love you when your body changes?

Before I proposed to Ruth, I tried to honestly imagine how I would respond if she was severely disfigured in an accident or gained a lot of weight. Would I still love her? That was a tough question to consider since I was so taken by her beauty. I would not choose to marry a woman to whom I was not attracted.

That question becomes even harder for a guy to evaluate if sex is in the relationship. Sex is so pleasurable that he cannot determine if he is in love with the woman as a person or if he is in love with sex and her physical appearance. Most guys are not very skilled at introspection. Analyzing their feelings with this difficult brain teaser is especially tough. Unfortunately, you are the one creating the impossible evaluation by having sex with him. If it turns out that it was the sex and your nice body he was in love with instead of your personality, you may be waving goodbye one day with a stretch-mark-inducing baby on your hip as he drives off to meet someone with fewer bulges.

Chapter 35

Boyfriend Bait— Guaranteed to Work

AS I MENTIONED before, I toured Europe one summer with a couple of college friends. We had backpacks and train passes so we could go anywhere we wanted. Many beautiful castles, cathedrals, and country-sides are etched in my memory from that trip. Another memory from Amsterdam is etched in my mind, but it's not beautiful.

Amsterdam is a city where prostitution is legal. My friends and I decided we wanted to see this for ourselves, so one evening we headed to the red light district. None of us had a shred of interest in visiting a prostitute—only seeing this part of society. It was definitely the seedy side of town, but lots of people were there and many tourists walked the streets just like us. The prostitutes I remember sat on stools in storefront windows. They sat where merchandise normally would be displayed for window shoppers. We were horrified at the sights. Many of the prostitutes were overweight, older women with leathery, wrinkled skin, thin hair, tattoos, and were smoking cigarettes. They were positively grotesque; there was nothing sensual about them. We left the district with a sickening sense of empty lives and the hopelessness that must follow women involved with these activities.

Although a million dollars and a hazmat suit would not have induced me to touch one of those ladies, obviously, many men were so desperate for sex, they would pay to be with these women.

Lesson Learned:

1. Some men will do *anything* to get sex.
2. A female who will provide sex or sexual activities is guaranteed to be able to find a male who is interested.

In Amsterdam, the men pay their money and go behind the curtain with the ugly prostitute to have sex. In America, the boy only needs to say, "I love you. You are pretty. You are my girlfriend. Let's hook up." No money changes hands and they head to somebody's house to have sex. Plenty of guys cannot walk away from that deal. The majority of girls seem to be falling for it. High schoolers, Hollywood celebrities, college co-eds, professional women: all seem to be fine with the deal.

I have the same empathy and heartache for the women of Amsterdam as I do for the women of America. Both groups of women have been duped by society into believing that having sex is what they are supposed to do and must do to get a man. They think it is OK because the guy is well groomed, articulate, kind, and different from the rest. "Everything is under control. After all, he loves me." Eventually, now or five years into the marriage, the woman concludes that he is not, "different from the rest."

Chapter 36

All Men Are Sex Maniacs

Not Quite True

THIS TITLE IS not quite true, but it is close enough to the truth that you could make that assumption about any guy with whom you hang out. Movie stars, athletes, celebrities, pastors, toads, princes, me—it doesn't matter who you list—virtually all men are sex maniacs. Unless they are tooling around a retirement village in a wheelchair with one wheel in the grave, you can assume that sexual thoughts are on men's minds or on close standby. We come packaged that way—no assembly or batteries required. Men spend much more time thinking about females and sex than most girls, wives, and women would believe. (Women think about relationships.) Some research says that males think about sex in some way about every two minutes. That frequency might be debatable, but clearly men think about sex much more than women do and can shift to sexual thoughts in the blink of an eye. Blame it on testosterone. It is true. The important consideration is what each man does about it. What reason does a man have to refrain from pursuing his sexual urges? Construction workers may hoot and whistle if a pretty girl walks by. Bankers in suits look, but they do it with banker-like discretion. Sexual attraction is universal. (Note: Stress, fatigue, personal issues, past influences, some medical conditions, and individual uniqueness can create exceptions to the sex maniac rule.)

I have talked with groups of Christian men who sincerely believe that it is a sin against God to contemplate having sex with a woman who is not their wife. Intellectually, morally, and spiritually, they are against it. Yet, in honest conversation most will say that sexual urges are among the toughest struggles they face in trying to do the right thing. A Christian man is just as tempted as any other man by pornography, short skirts, cleavage, and smiling friendly women.

If a man does not have a higher authority, firmly held religious reasons, or a moral/ethical belief system that would call on him to show sexual restraint, you had better watch out. If he is unable and uninterested in showing restraint now while you are dating, don't expect that he will suddenly develop a reliable moral system that would constrain his sexual interests to just his wife—whenever he gets married. That is why a man's sexual actions and beliefs are such a reliable indicator of the type of husband he would be.

Once married, that insatiable sex drive is part of the magic glue that keeps couples together with men chasing their wives for a lifetime. If he is a good husband, the wife loves to get caught. If he is a poor husband, he may be chasing other women or pornographic images.

Ironically, nationally recognized sex therapists Dr. Clifford and Joyce Penner say half the couples who seek sexual therapy because of lessened desire report that it is the husband who lacks desire. Men can leave their wives unfulfilled if they divert their sexual energy to pornagraphy, an affair, self-gratification, or work. Although men usually have a high sex drive, problems in the marriage relationship will automatically affect the sex life.

"A great lover is a man who can keep one woman
satisfied for a lifetime."

—Unknown

Chapter 37

Women Want Sex
As Much As Men

ALTHOUGH I HAVE just described the hypersexual nature of men, I was recently watching television when a young adult actress made the statement, "Women want sex just as much as men." Her statement caused me to consider if she was right. While her comment was inspired by the genuine intense yearnings that she feels, she underestimates the male sex drive when compared to the female's. She was mostly correct with her statement, but she was slightly confused regarding what she really wants compared to what men want. Men want the physical pleasure of sex. They may want a true relationship too, but they are driven by their nature to pursue physical pleasure. Women may want sex, but they are driven by their nature to be loved, cherished, protected, and desired by a man. When a woman is having sex, she may *feel* loved, cherished, protected, and desired, but these emotions are artificial and temporary if there is no lifetime commitment. She mistakes the counterfeit emotions she feels during sex with the real thing. The female mind assumes that since she's involved in the sex act, it must be true that the man loves and desires her, but the male mind can desire her sexually with little attraction to the actual person. Women get burned all the time because they do not understand this important differentiation.

Ultimately, men and women are similar in their yearning for oneness with a soul mate; the complete connection of heart, mind, body, and soul. The actress would have been correct if she said, "Women want oneness just as much as men do." The key to remember is that it is easy for men to do sex without oneness.

Chapter 38

A Million Dollar Bowl of Cheerios®

THERE IS A PBS program entitled the *Traveling Antiques Road Show* in which people bring miscellaneous artwork and furniture from their houses for an appraisal. The highlight of the show is always when someone presents some worthless looking bowl she almost sold in a garage sale and finds out it is worth a million dollars because Napoleon made it in his kindergarten class.

Now, imagine you give that precious bowl to your daughter as her inheritance when she moves out of the home. You tell her what it is worth and she is very happy. Some time later, a male friend visiting her tells her that it is just an ordinary bowl. He decides to eat his Cheerios® in it and carelessly drops it on the floor. No big deal. It was just a bowl. He had no appreciation for her precious, one-of-a-kind treasure. "Don't you have another bowl?" he says aimlessly. "Pass the milk."

Every woman has a precious commodity—her sexuality. You must know it, believe it, and protect it like you would a million dollar bowl. Most of our culture is trying to convince you that you are not really all that valuable. In fact, many men would like to use you for their very ordinary and selfish purposes. They will casually put their Cheerios® (or sperm) in your bowl. Harsh but true. It is no great loss to them if the valuable bowl is broken or your valuable sexuality is used cheaply. They have little to lose, and you have much at stake.

This breakfast scenario illustrates the huge difference between what is at stake for a man, compared to the potential emotional and physical consequences for a woman when they share sexual activity. Men obviously want women to think it is no big deal. Women may try to justify their actions by denying that they were hurt. After awhile they can be so numb, it doesn't seem to matter any more. Remember, sex is great! The last thing you want in the realm of your sexuality is numbness, yet some women think they can handle sex as lightly as men can. It's just not true; the numbness will set in, affecting you right now and even later in your future marriage.

Our culture will tell you that you are crazy if you do not put that fine china to use. Why leave it on the shelf unused? "Give me a bowl of Cheerios®. I want it now." Isn't that romantic?

Chapter 39

Women Have Been Duped

I HAVE SEEN a skit in which several girls are brought on stage blindfolded and then are instructed that they are racing against the others to accomplish some rather embarrassing task. One by one, the blindfolds are removed until only one naïve girl is frantically working alone at the task while the entire audience laughs at her expense. Eventually, she figures it out and quits—humiliated. She believed what she had been told about the purpose of the game but she was duped.

Society has gradually been duping women with the same trick, but most women do not even know it. You still have the blindfold on and are feverishly doing all the things society tells you must be done if you want to catch a man. The men are hooting to cheer you on because you are giving them a great show. You are giving them all they want. *They* certainly will not tell you to stop.

Let me explain the progression that has seeped into our society and left women with that empty, exploited feeling when the blindfold comes off and they realize they have been duped by the entire culture. In the case of relationships, girls are duped one boy at a time with the assistance of the rest of society.

A young woman trying to figure out how she should behave with men looks around for clues. She sees Hollywood celebrities routinely sleeping together on screen and off. Sitcoms discuss sex casually. Her friends are having sex with their boyfriends.

Most modern media make the following assumptions:

- Most normal people are fine with the idea of a woman having sex with a boyfriend.
- No good reason exists to deny a woman the pleasure of sex.
- Sex is the only way to get a man.
- Consequences such as STDs, pregnancy, broken relationships, divorce are rare.

The most likeable stars who we want to emulate often sleep together in the movies. They seem so mature, confident, beautiful, romantic, and perfectly matched. We assume that they will get married and live happily ever after. Most romantic movies end when the man and woman finally get together because that is the most exciting moment for everyone. Let's end on a high note while everyone is happy.

Media has become the primary source of information and wisdom for many people. If sleeping with your date works for celebrities, it must be a good way to go.

Remember, the purpose of movie makers is to sell tickets to movies—not to improve your relationships and marriage. Hollywood produces what people will pay to see. We like to watch passion and imagine ourselves in the romantic situation of the movie. We enjoy the fantasy and don't understand that movies are often not the way life really happens.

There is an old story about a little girl who usually wore a skirt to school. One day, she told her mother that every day, the boys pay her 10 cents to climb the pole. The mother explained that the boys were just doing that so they could see her underwear. The next day, the mother asked her how it went with the pole. The little girl said she got even with the boys. Today she didn't wear underwear.

Many women today are as confused as the little girl about their sexual standards. Women are giving it away for free while men are enjoying it and coming to expect it. Over the last few decades, a huge shift has taken place in the way women view their sexuality, and most women have no idea that they have been totally duped.

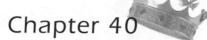

Chapter 40

The Physics of Sex

"With great power comes great responsibility."
—Ben Parker *(Spiderman's Uncle)*

TAP A BALL lightly and it will roll a short distance. Club it with a baseball bat and it could fly out of the park. A larger action creates a larger consequence. If a freight train hits a car in its path, it will demolish the car and push it a mile or so. When a bullet leaves a gun, the gun recoils in the opposite direction. One of Sir Isaac Newton's laws of physics teaches us that for every action, there is an equal and opposite reaction. Interestingly, this law is equally true in the world of sex. Any way you slice it, sexual intercourse is the pinnacle of human pleasure. Nothing else a person experiences can equal the electrifying sensation and ultimate ecstasy of sexual intercourse when it is done the way it was designed to be done.

Most people are quite familiar with the power and pleasure of sex because our culture promotes sex all around us every day. It must be special if it gets that much attention. Unfortunately, Sir Newton's law is in effect. Counterbalancing its potential to produce ultimate pleasure is the predictable ability of sex to produce ultimate pain and destruction—especially for women. Isaac and I did not make up these laws; we only observe them and describe what we see. It does not matter if we agree or disagree with the laws—that's just the way it is.

After watching an apple fall from a tree, Mr. Newton was also quite interested in gravity. The law of gravity is similar to the third law of physics. If you climb a tree and ignore the law of gravity, you will likely fall out of the tree and be injured. You can be unaware of the law, disagree with the law, or consider the law to be unfair, but if you ignore the law, you could end up with a broken arm. So it is with the law of physics as it pertains to sex. If we ignore the law, we will likely experience the painful consequences.

Sex can be the glue that keeps a married couple unified as one or it can be the dynamite that destroys the relationship and leaves a lifetime of pain. We have become so casual about sex that we have fooled ourselves into believing that the dynamite in our hands is just a box of chocolate. Most people do not seem to even acknowledge that there may be some very real consequences to every action we take, especially when it comes to sex.

A young girl is molested. A teenage girl hates herself when she realizes that her boyfriend did not love her at all but just wanted sexual favors from her. A wife is forced to do acts that are repugnant to her. Do not be fooled by the trivial happy face our media places on sex. Abusing the most potent substance known to mankind can lead to the most devastating consequences known. That is the wisdom we all learned as Spiderman's uncle spoke his last profound words. "With great power comes great responsibility." If you are a woman, you have a lot more power than Spiderman. If you unleash your superpower at the wrong time, you are much more likely to be the one who suffers than the man you were with.

Chapter 41

"You Would Do Just Fine."

MANY GUYS (TOADS) are aimlessly wandering through life, looking for a place to deposit their sperm and you would do just fine for that purpose. A crass statement, but true. The only requirement is a willing recipient. Much toad energy is directed to this mission in life, especially among males in the 14 to 24-year-old range. The hormones are peaking, they're playing sports, looking buff, and are often around many girls in this stage of life.

All are not aimlessly wandering in this pursuit. Some are quite strategic, maneuvering through adolescence with carefully planned lines and actions that they know will work on many girls. Whether aimless or strategic, the results are the same. All of these guys know that the magic passwords are, "I love you" because love is what girls are truly after. "I love you," translated from toad language, may actually mean, "You would do just fine."

Chapter 42

"The Girls All Get Prettier at Closing Time"

JERRY LEE LEWIS (FROM A WITTY AND REVEALING COUNTRY SONG)

FOR MANY MEN, their top priority in life is finding a woman who is willing to have sex or provide sexual activity. To them, everything else is secondary. The song represented by the title above is about some men's attitude at a club, bar, party, etc. They begin the evening with high hopes for finding a beautiful woman with whom they could go out and have sex. As the evening progresses, they begin to realize that they have not connected with any of the beautiful women, so they start to lower their standards from a ten down to a one. Personality and character are never mentioned. Once the beauty criterion is abandoned, the only requirement remaining is that she is female and willing to have sex.

Part of the song is humorous because we all understand the reality check that happens when we must shift our expectations from dreams to realities. The sad part of this song illustrates that for many men, the woman is just a piece of meat—a sexual outlet. Any man with this attitude is the bottom of the barrel, pond-scum-variety toad. In most party/club environments, you are surrounded by them. Your hope of finding a prince there becomes a dangerous, needle-in-a-haystack search among so many toxic toads.

The irony is virtually every man and woman in the room ultimately has the same goal. They want to find a wonderful, lovely, interesting spouse who will love and cherish them; share dreams, struggles, and

129

innermost thoughts; raise children; and have a regular diet of passionate sex; but they have all been tragically sidetracked by that last item on the list. The sex drive and fear of loneliness have taken over rational thought and put them into desperation mode. They look confident, smooth, and hip, but inside they are dying of fear and loneliness. Look at the tabloids filled with celebrity breakups and you will see that they are as desperate as the common person. The insanity crosses all socio-economic barriers.

Chapter 43

"You Can't Handle the Truth"

AS SNARLED AT TOM CRUISE BY JACK NICHOLSON IN *A FEW GOOD MEN*

YOU THINK YOU can handle your drives, but you underestimate the mind-warping power of sex. The truth is, "You can't handle the pleasure." People who are otherwise rational and sensible in every other part of their lives lose it when it comes to relationships. A person with a sane life and career does not necessarily make sane decisions regarding intimacy. People assume that they can keep the sexual parts of their lives under control because they have done so with every other part of their lives.

The pleasure of intimacy is like a drug; you get a little and you want more. The slippery slope in the quest for more can take you to a point of no return. A song in *Phantom of the Opera* called "The Point of No Return" addresses this very issue. The point of no return is when instinct and pleasure start to kick in and rational thought disappears. Even if you had no intention of ending up with intimate sexual contact, you suddenly find yourself there. You can't understand why you are powerless to walk away. This pull is quite foreign to you because every other part of your life is so rational. How could you possibly lose the power to walk away? The reason is because you grossly underestimate the power of sex and you grossly overestimate your willpower. You give yourself way too much credit for being sensible, which is a universal flaw in everyone—not just you. However, most of society does not even acknowledge any reason to resist.

If a woman is unaware of her slow "crockpot" nature, she is unprepared for the emotional momentum that builds when there is genuine mutual affection with a great guy. Part of you thinks "no" but another part of you *feels* "yes." When you move into uncharted emotional/sensual territory with strong conflicting emotions, you may not be thinking clearly. All of the cautions that you intellectually agree with suddenly seem less significant in the heat of the moment. Yet, all of the consequences remain. I say again, you can't handle the pleasure.

Chapter 44

Why Women Do Not
Play in the NFL

I WAS RECENTLY talking to the mother of a 14-year-old boy who was playing football at school for his first season. I asked her how he was liking it. She said, "It's perfect for him. He gets to push and shove as hard as he wants. In fact, the coaches teach him specifically how to hit lower and harder. Every day, he is wrestling guys to the ground and he loves it. I don't know why, but he loves it."

This woman's son loves it because he is a boy. Boys and men love to wrestle each other, push the limits, and sweat. We think of a game as a battle because we are warriors and conquerors. We anticipate the opportunity for glory by making a great play in front of the whole school. We are willing to sacrifice our time and bodies for these simple pleasures.

This mentality does not generally appeal to girls. If a woman played in the NFL, she could get crushed or killed on the first play. Yes, I know there are exceptions. My point is that everyone acknowledges that girls are different from boys physically. Many people, however, deny that there is a huge difference in the way the two sexes think and respond to life. Relationally, this is a disastrous mistake.

You Can't Have Sex Like a Man

If a woman enters a sexual relationship thinking she can think and act like a man, she is just as sure to get injured as a woman playing for the Redskins. She can deny it all she wants, but once she gets in the game, the injury is just a matter of time. The only questions are how long until it happens and what injury it will be?

Chapter 45

Men Are Waffles, Women Are Spaghetti

BILL AND PAM Farrel wrote an entire book called **Men Are Like Waffles, Women Are Like Spaghetti** (Harvest House Publishers, 2001) based on the following edible analogy.

Waffles

Waffles have lots of compartments. You can load them with syrup one square at a time, by row, or by just pouring your syrup anywhere. Everyone has his own technique which may vary with the mood at breakfast time. To place syrup in one compartment and not affect the other compartments is easy. Men are compartmentalized like waffles; one part of the life does not necessarily affect the other parts. Men can have a bad day but go play a sport and completely forget about it for that time. Men can argue all morning in a business meeting and go out to lunch together with no problem. Men prefer to focus on one thing at a time: watching a football game, fixing the light switch, brain surgery, etc. They like tasks and can often compartmentalize or separate them like the squares in a waffle. It is neither good nor bad; it's just the way men are generally.

Men are especially compartmentalized in the area of sex. In fact, it is a compartment that is especially impervious to actions in other parts of the waffle. A guy can have sex and can keep it in one little square of

135

his waffle-like brain. With some exceptions, a guy's interest in sex is not altered by other events in his life. If he gets the promotion, he wants sex. If he gets fired he wants sex. Happy, sad, mad, sore, tired—it doesn't really matter. The sex drive is still there.

Obviously, severe stresses in a man's life can blot out interest in sex, but that is more the exception than the rule. Emotions do not need to be linked to the sexual pleasure for a man because sex is much more physical than emotional. If a guy has sex with a girl and she decides to end the relationship, the fact that they had sex does not really create much extra heartache for him. If anything, he probably thinks, "Well, at least I got to have sex." His biggest regret may be that he won't have sex again with this girl. He does not have emotional regret that he gave away a precious part of himself or that he took a precious part from her.

Spaghetti

Women are an entirely different plate of food. A plate of spaghetti is a tangle of twisted strands that are impossible to follow from end to end. It is such a complicated mass that you could never know which strand is which. As a female, you are most likely good at multi-tasking. Moms can talk on the phone, fix dinner, and help with homework simultaneously. Business women can do three things at once. Maybe you can text your friends, do homework, and watch TV at the same time. The female mind is fully integrated and oriented toward relationships. Events that happen in one part of your life are likely to have some effect in another part of your life. All of these aspects of life are interconnected like the spaghetti on the plate. You cannot put sauce on just one noodle and not get it on others.

Nobody, not even you, understands the complex female mind. It is no better and no worse than the male mind; it's just different. The sexual component of the feminine mind is even more mysterious and impossible to untangle, but a few traits are common to all women. A woman's sexuality is linked in complex ways to the other parts of her life. Whether you like it or not, your emotions are inseparable from sexual activity. Most women would want or need to be emotionally tied to a man before sexual activity occurs. Women must at least think a relationship exists before she is willing to have sex, or she believes that by having sex, she will get the love relationship she craves.

If a couple has sex, and the man decides to break it off, the woman feels as if she has been used. She can try to take it like a man and pretend she is unaffected, yet, no matter how hard she tries, her emotions are linked with the sex. Self-esteem plummets. To the casual observer who encounters her at school or work, she may look completely normal and unaffected, but inside she is falling apart. Contrast that with the man who is glad that he at least got some sex out of the relationship. Huge, huge difference.

You Can't Have Sex Like a Man

Any woman who claims she has separated her emotions from sex has made a ghastly mutilation of her sexuality. She has tried to have sex like a man and it cannot be done. This separation is easy for the man and impossible for the woman. A woman who has taken the drastic step of shutting down her emotions creates lifetime scars and consequences that can follow her into marriage. She thinks she knows and controls her sexual attitude and responses, but now things are even more complicated than the plate of spaghetti. The experience winds its way through her sensitive, intuitive brain and penetrates to her core. To predict the endpoint of any particular strand of spaghetti is impossible just as it is impossible to predict how sexual activity will affect the other areas of her life. One thing is easy to predict; she indeed will be affected.

Non-consenting sexual experiences such as molestation or rape can have devastating, long-term effects because the whole person, not just the sexual organs, is affected by the crime. It could be years later in marriage that the effects resurface and the wound is re-opened. Sexually violent acts cause more than an isolated injury or momentary pain; they can have a lifetime effect on the entire woman.

Chapter 46

Numbed

SOME HORSE TRADERS are notorious for being dishonest. They use sly tricks to cover the lameness in a horse just long enough to make the sale and get out of town. Let me share with you a numbing trick that can also be a legitimate veterinary procedure. Yes, this will apply to sex eventually. Remember, I am a vet.

If a horse is lame, a vet can place a nerve block at strategic places to help pinpoint where the problem is. When nerves in the lower leg are injected with anesthetic, the horse can no longer feel anything below that point. If the horse limped because of a sore hoof, it suddenly looks normal with no limp because the pain has been blocked. By injecting anesthetic into the nerves in the leg, a vet can sometimes determine where the problem is and begin treatment. Once the injection wears off, the horse goes back to limping. If the pain persists, it is possible to "nerve" the horse which means to permanently block the nerve so the horse will never feel anything in its hoof again. "Nerving" is only done when everything else has failed because the horse is more likely to stumble and injure the foot more because the foot has no feeling.

If a woman has been sexually active and repeatedly injured by relationships that let her down, she must do something to deal with the pain. One method to relieve the pain is to create emotional barriers, mentally blocking out the emotional pain or learning to separate herself from her sexuality. Emotional numbness can seem better than excruciating emotional pain. Blocking out the pain can allow a woman to continue with life and even continue being sexually active without true emotions. It may help her survival, but if she does get married, she has been emotionally "nerved," perhaps making it impossible for her husband to please her, no matter how good he is. Complete emotional freedom is a necessity for a wife's maximum enjoyment. Numbness is not the adjective you want to use to describe a lifetime of intimacy with your husband. The problem can be overcome, but unless it is overcome, this numbness can be serious baggage to lug through the marriage.

Chapter 47

I Can't Get No Satisfaction

MICK JAGGER, THE ROLLING STONES

Wisdom from the Stones

MICK GOT IT right. He *can't* get no satisfaction. He tries and he tries and he tries and he tries, but he can't. The farther a person moves from a single exclusive lifetime committed relationship with a single sexual partner, the harder it becomes to trust others and stay satisfied with your partner. This dynamic is important to know now while you are single, because actions that you and your future husband do now (even if you have not met yet) will affect your ability to stay satisfied with each other as you grow old together.

Satisfaction is a struggle for us in many parts of our lives, so why would it be any different in marriage? We are not satisfied with our television. We need a bigger, flatter screen. We want a better lawn, bigger house, newer car, better job, better teacher, better clothes, better body, better everything, including a better spouse. Staying satisfied is a fundamental struggle in staying committed and happily married. After a while, husbands and wives are tempted to look around and think that other spouses or singles are better looking, more helpful, more fun, more responsible. "I could have done better. I no longer love my spouse. I will allow myself to consider an affair or divorce." This feeling is not deliberate; dissatisfaction just seeps in.

If you have brought relationship baggage into your marriage or used your one piece of duct tape with others before using it with your spouse, you will be more likely to feel dissatisfied and more willing to walk away from the marriage. Remember, a fresh piece of duct tape ripping the hair off your arm the first time will hurt a lot more than the second time that same piece is ripped from your arm. If you have walked away once, it is easier to walk away again. We see this in divorce stats. The first time you are married, you have a 50% probability of divorce. People marrying for the second time have a 70% chance of divorce, and third marriages have an 80% chance of divorce. Each time you walk away, it becomes easier to do it the next time.

What you do in your singleness will affect your married life.

Compare and Contrast

We can fall into the trap of comparing who we have with who we have known in the past or with someone else we know now. Have you ever been at a restaurant and your entrée is placed in front of you and you are excited about your meal? A few moments later, the waiter brings out another person's order that looks more scrumptious than the one you ordered. You experience entrée envy as you wish you had ordered the other meal.

Our exposure to a selection of entrées can make us less satisfied with the entrée we have. So it goes with sexual partners. Exposure to a selection of sexual partners can make us less satisfied with our spouse. Remember, the intensity of sexual experiences causes those memories to lock into our perma-memory so they are always available for comparisons. Note that memories of previous non-sexual relationships do not have the same unshakable effect as sexual relationships. Your spouse might have seemed perfectly wonderful if he was the only person you have been intimate with, but compare and contrast can lead to dissatisfaction for the husband or the wife.

Chapter 48

Single Sex vs. Married Sex

"Women get married hoping their husband will change. Men get
married hoping their wife will not change."
—Unknown

IF YOU DESIGNED a love potion to make a man and woman fall and
stay madly in love with each other for their entire lives, you would need a
powerful concoction. I suggest sex be an indispensable ingredient. There
are a number of characteristics of sex that make it perfect for maintaining
a lifetime married relationship. Unfortunately, those same characteristics
almost always have an opposite and negative effect on single people—a
treacherous irony. Here is a rundown on these characteristics.

Sex Causes Blindness

The pleasure of sex is so intense, people are willing to overlook
incredible flaws in the other person. The flaws may be obvious to every
other person on earth, but the couple having sex may not see the flaws at
all. For married couples, overlooking flaws is important because we are all
loaded with flaws and the flaws become more obvious the more we really
know each other. In marriage, you can't hide much for long. The thrill of a
good marriage is that your spouse knows your flaws intimately and chooses

to overlook them and love you as you are. Since a wife cannot repair the flaws in her husband, she had better be prepared to live with them.

Now contrast that to the problems this blindness creates for single people who have sex. Once again, the intense pleasure causes the couple to overlook significant problems with each other. If you are with a guy because you think he might be a possible husband, you will want to have an accurate picture of him to help you make a wise life decision. Likewise, you would want him to know who you really are and be fully satisfied with you. People are complex creatures. It takes a long time and a lot of effort to truly get to know someone. Once you throw the blinders of sex into the mix, the fuzzy picture of the relationship will be much harder to discern. Eventually, your vision will clear. If you sleep with him before you are married, the soft focus can make him look appealing for a while, but you might wake up one morning after you are married and suddenly see crystal clear—a toad lying beside you. Ribbit!

Ben Franklin gave lots of good advice. He even mentioned relational blindness. He said, "Everyone should enter marriage with their eyes wide open and remain married with their eyes half shut." To follow Ben's advice, you would want to keep your vision and judgment in peak condition while choosing your prince and enjoy the soft focus after you're married that makes even your imperfect husband look good to you. The older you get, the more thankful you will be that your husband also sees you through a soft-focus lens.

Oh, Oh! The Potion Is Wearing Off

The thrill of sex is temporary. In fact, for a guy (the microwave) the drop off in interest can be even faster than the arousal. He can go from the peak of passion to walking out the door in a heartbeat if the sex blinders fall off immediately. A woman who is caught up in the passion of the moment can have an instantaneous flood of regret when it is over. However, if neither party feels regret, they might just think, "When can we do that again?" A happily married couple will ask that question. An unmarried couple may or may not. If there was no regret, you can bet that is the question on their mind—especially the guy's. This leads us to our next sexual trait—insatiability.

I Can't Get Enough of Your Love

The sex drive is insatiable. The pleasure and satisfaction never last, so people always come back for more. For married couples the insatiable nature of sex is important because intercourse provides the deepest form of intimacy that humans can experience. It unifies a couple in a way that no other activity can. The unquenchable drive keeps couples coming back together time after time for their entire lives, always strengthening the bond that the stresses of the world try to break down. Although some wives may complain about their husband's insatiable sex drive, they should be glad that he is always coming back for more. The alternative is not good in a marriage.

Now contrast that effect on an unmarried couple. Unless it is a bad experience or filled with regret, a couple will almost certainly want to have sex again. The insatiable nature of sex insists that a couple will continue to have sex until they break up or unless they take radical measures to break the cycle. Since the male sex drive is considerably more insatiable than the female's, the man would find it to be nearly impossible to refrain from pressing for more sex unless he has an ethical or moral reason to refrain. Without a rational plan and supernatural help, I would bet that sex will overpower good intentions either immediately or eventually.

More Fun Than a Human Should Be Allowed

Sex is the most intense, most pleasurable, mutual, simultaneous experience humans can enjoy. What a great deal for married folks—a lifetime of ecstasy. But what a tough situation for singles. This intense pleasure just doesn't linger outside waiting for us; it is calling to us from every part of our culture. Virtually anyone can experience sex if he or she is willing. Our greatest pleasure is also our greatest temptation. Whether you actively pursue sex or accidentally fall into it, the detrimental effects on your dream to find a prince for life cannot be separated from the act. You can make serious mistakes and still find a great husband. Some mistakes, however, will bring extra challenges and pain that follow you for a long time.

The Thrill Is Gone

Sex is powerful. It can carry an empty relationship for quite a while but eventually, its power will wane. If sex is the primary glue holding the couple together, the relationship will crumble when the thrill wears off. It might keep the couple entertained long enough to marry each other, but it cannot hold anyone together long term. Lifetime togetherness is accomplished with love, sacrifice, and commitment. Sex helps to seal the deal, but without the foundation of love and commitment, it is doomed. Sex makes a good marriage great, but it makes a bad marriage terrible. The difficulty is that the thrill of love is easily confused with the thrill of sex and the couple may have trouble discerning if love is really the foundation of their relationship. You can end up wasting some of your prime time with a dead-end relationship or, worse yet, marry a guy who is really a poor choice for you.

A Little Less Talk and a Lot More Action

Sex enables a couple to communicate the deepest form of intimacy— even beyond words. For a married couple committed to each other for a lifetime, the intimacy and knowledge of one another can grow as the relationship grows. Oddly, for an unmarried couple trying to get to know one another, sex has the opposite affect. Obviously, during sex, the couple will *feel* intimate; however, sex will actually hinder communication. While you want to build the relationship and decide if you would want to marry this man, making out is much easier, more exciting, and more pleasurable than conversation.

Before a couple has sex, both people put a lot of time and effort into getting to know each other, impressing each other, doing things together, and generally building the relationship. Once sex enters the picture, the communication process is short-circuited—especially for the man. You might still be very interested in conversing, but he is very interested in picking up where you left off last time you were together. Even the best prince will struggle to keep his mind on you-the-person rather than you-the-body once you have shared sexual intimacy. He might be politely talking with you, but in the back of his mind, he is thinking about later. This is the way men think when sex is one of the options for the night. When a happily married husband and wife go on a romantic getaway, you can bet that the wife is looking forward to the undivided attention of her man, heart-to-heart conversations, and relationship-building while she feels cherished in the romantic setting. The husband will certainly enjoy the evening, but his highlight is when the talking stops. The married couple hopefully already has a solid foundation on which their marriage sits. The unmarried couple is hoping to build a foundation for marriage but sex will repeatedly divert them from the genuine communication needed to get to know all the facets of each other.

Chicken or the Egg

No one knows which came first. Nobody really cares about the order, but sometimes order matters. When it comes to sex and building a relationship, the order matters. It is critical to build relationship and evaluate the husband potential of the man you're dating *before* sex enters the picture. If you try to build and evaluate the relationship after sex is in the mix, the relational growth will be slower and your evaluation will be skewed.

Fast Food or Gourmet?

Kids love fast food. No waiting; choose what you want; tastes good but might be bad for you; few rules; leave the table and get whatever you need; unlimited soda refills. It all seems fun and exciting to them and they always want to go back. Contrast that with a five-star gourmet restaurant. Kids are too immature to appreciate the quality. An adult would savor the atmosphere and marvel at the unusual entrées. Appetizers, fine wine, filet mignon, death by chocolate—the exquisite experience would be fully appreciated. The quality comparison between these two meals is similar to the quality comparison between single sex and married sex (in a strong, healthy, marriage). To a single person, sex may seem thrilling—just like a Big Mac® tastes good, but, in reality, sex while single only scratches the surface compared to the gourmet experience of sex within marriage. Don't settle for a happy meal when you could have filet mignon.

The chart below summarizes the contrasting results of sex in marriage compared to sex outside of marriage.

Necessary characteristics	Marriage	Single
Great pleasure needed to draw couples together.	Most intense, most pleasurable, mutual, simultaneous experience humans can enjoy.	The greatest pleasure is the most powerful temptation.
Blinding	Overlook flaws in spouse, willing to live with irritating traits.	Overlook serious flaws while dating/courting to create a skewed evaluation of the relationship.
Temporary	Married couples are never satisfied. The thrill does not last so they always come back for more. Insatiable sex drive. Always looking forward to the next time.	Temporary thrill wears off. Want more. Repeat mistakes. Like hunger. Never provides the lasting satisfaction we crave.
Permabond	Intended to be permanent with only one person	Breaking a permanent bond is painful and damaging
Sex follows relationship. Sex is powerful but has limitations.	Sex cannot carry a relationship long term. Love and commitment must carry the load. Sex follows relationship. Sex makes a good marriage great. Makes bad marriage terrible.	Sex can carry a relationship long enough to cause a poor choice of spouse or keep you away from better princes. The thrill wears off without love and commitment.
Exquisite quality	5 star gourmet meal	Happy meal

More Contrasts

Appreciated vs. Evaluated

Single—He appreciates the sex. Does he appreciate you? Your body and your performance are being evaluated.

Married—He appreciates you *and* the sex.

Comparisons vs. No Competition

Single—If he is sleeping with you, who else has he slept with? How do you measure up?

Married—You are it. Nothing to compare.

Self-conscious vs. Confident

Single—Of course you will be self-conscious if you are naked before a man who has no commitment to you and is undoubtledly evaluating your body and your performance.

Women struggle with self-doubt about themselves and their bodies. Married or single—it's universal. Women need to be reassured that they are desirable.

Married—A good husband helps to relieve his wife's self-doubt by his perpetual admiration and affirmation of her. Men like to look at naked women. If you are his wife and the only naked woman he sees, he fixates on you and genuinely admires you—even though you may not feel beautiful. Lifetime commitment creates security and confidence for you.

Uncertainty vs. Security

Single—You have no idea where you are headed. He can ditch you tomorrow.

Married—A lifetime vow. He will be there tomorrow. You are totally accepted and secure.

Love and Sex Can Cause Similar Effects

The physical forces of sex can be tightly intertwined and confused with the power of love. A relationship is so complex and important that you must evaluate it carefully to determine if you have been overcome by emotion and physical attraction or if there is truly a solid foundation there of love.

Chapter 49

"What's Love Got to Do with It?"

TINA TURNER

IN SPITE OF all the discussion about sex and its effects, love is still king. Love can survive entirely on its own. It is the most powerful, noble, spiritual component of humans. Love causes many of the same effects as sex, but love is universally good—dating or married—anytime, anywhere. The similarities between sex and love are so close that in many minds they are virtually interchangeable. The confusion is understandable considering much of our common terminology. Making love, give me some love, love for sale, and love child are all common phrases that actually have to do with having sex. No wonder people are confused.

Love Is Euphoric

If we were to add love to our chart in the previous chapter, we would show that love causes the most intense *emotional* pleasure humans can experience compared to the most intense *physical* pleasure of sex. When a man and woman fall in love, they are genuinely euphoric. The grass looks greener, the birds sing louder, and the future looks brighter.

Love Is Blind

Love can cause blindness just like sex can. People who genuinely love each other choose to overlook the shortcomings of their partner. A

151

woman can fall in love with a guy and be blind to his faults regardless of their sexual contact.

Temporary Love

True love is permanent. Unfortunately, in spite of our best intentions, our love often falls short of its high calling. Without warning, selfishness or impatience will jump in and impede our actions of genuine love. Although we expect love to be permanent when we say "I do," in reality, love is an ongoing decision. Love has nothing to do with how we feel; it is a decision we make when we wake up each morning. "I choose to love my spouse whether he/she deserves it or not." Your other option, which is more common, is to say to yourself, "I choose to love my spouse IF he or she is good to me." This attitude is not true love. Do not confuse the warm fuzzy feelings of love with love itself. Feelings ebb and flow. The initial euphoria will subside and then you can settle into a more subdued sense of well-being. However, those nice feelings will be challenged in times of disappointment, anger, irritation, and uncertainty; and they will be strengthened in times of humor, bliss, and peace. In other words, the entire spectrum of human emotion comes into play when love is concerned. The repeated decision to love another through all of these emotions is what makes love last.

> *The repeated decision to love another person through all of these emotions is what makes love last.*

Love Is Intended to Be Permanent

Parents' love for their children is perhaps the best example of permanent love. Our children may frustrate us, embarrass us, or disappoint us, but most parents still feel a bond of love for their children that transcends all of the difficulties.

True Love Is the Foundation

Love is the foundation of the relationship. It carries the load without limitations. Love's foundational power is in sharp contrast to sex which is severely limited in its ability to sustain a relationship. A house will crumble sooner or later without a foundation and so will a relationship that is built upon sex rather than love.

A Working Definition of True Love

Love is very patient and kind, never jealous or envious, never boastful or proud, never selfish or rude. Love does not demand its own way. It is not irritable or touchy. It does not hold grudges and will hardly even notice when others do wrong. It is never glad about injustice but celebrates whenever truth wins out.[1] If you love someone you will be loyal to him no matter what the cost. You will always believe in him, and always expect the best from him.

That is true love and true love is never damaging—even for single people. Since we are imperfect and never quite live up to this noble definition, we do the best we can and endure the pain when we or our loved one falls short. Pain is a part of every relationship. The physical forces of sex can be tightly intertwined and confused with the power of love. If you get love and sex confused or put them in the wrong order, your pain level will rise.

Mr. Rogers, the gentle host of the classic children's program, understood love.

It's you I like,
It's not the things you wear.
It's not the way you do your hair,
But it's you I like.
The way you are right now
The way down deep inside you
Not the things that hide you
Not your diplomas …
They're just beside you.

But it's you I like,
Every part of you,
Your skin, your eyes, your feelings,
Whether old or new.
I hope that you'll remember
Even when you're feeling blue,
That it's you I like,
It's you yourself, it's you
It's you I like!
Mr. Rogers

Chapter 50

It's Just a Bunny

IN A CLASSIC ridiculous movie, *Monty Python and the Holy Grail*, there is a scene in which a supposedly horrible beast is guarding a cave. The knights have heard horror stories about its ferocity, having been told, "It has long claws and horrible fangs. It is a hideous monster," so they approach the cave with great fear and caution. But all they see is a little bunny hopping around in front of the cave. "It's just a bunny," the first knight says in a British accent filled with derision. He approaches the cave casually and the bunny leaps to his throat biting and killing the knight. More knights follow and are slaughtered by the fake-looking killer bunny. It is a classic moment in movie comedy.

Sex outside of marriage is like the bunny. It looks like a harmless, fuzzy thing that you would want to cuddle. It looks warm, friendly, and desirable. People who warn against the dangers of sex while single are usually considered radical nuts, out of step with modern times. The derision is similar to that of the knights just before they were slaughtered. Many people hear the warnings about premarital sex and think they are not susceptible to its powers. You are surrounded by movies, magazines, TV shows, and friends who all deal with dating sex as if it is a harmless little fluff ball, nothing but fun. Any negative consequences are ignored or laughed at. Everyone seems to think sex is "just a little bunny" until it is too late. Remember this analogy. It is one of the most accurate word pictures I know to describe sex outside of marriage.

155

Chapter 51

Porn

Ignore This Section at Your Own Risk

LET ME WARN you that this is one of the ugliest chapters in this book. This unpleasant topic is rarely discussed. What you read may change your view of many men, particularly those who will deny the truth of this chapter. You decide if what I write is true. If you conclude I have overblown the problem, proceed into a relationship at your own peril.

Pornography is a mystery to many women because women are not nearly as susceptible to it as men. For men, porn draws them in like a flame does a moth. Porn poisons the male mind but the female becomes the victim. You should pay attention to this or you will get burned. It is a serious problem. Comedians joke about it, but it's not funny.

Some Stats Intended to Frighten You

Pornography is a contributing factor in 50% of divorces. One study over a twelve-year period found 100% of sexual abuse cases involved pornography. Another study of 12,000 sexual assault cases against minor-age girls nationwide found that 98% involved pornography. The porn industry generates $10–14 *billion* every year, more than major league baseball, basketball, and football combined. Twenty-five percent of all porn sites involve children and the number of sites increased from

30,000 to 300,000 in the last six years. Porn sites comprise 60% of all websites and attract thirty million Americans every day.[2]

I will describe the inner workings of the male mind and pornography. Remember, the male response to pornography is driven by the fact that virtually all men have a natural, instinctive, powerful sex drive. The question is: What do they do about it?

Without a moral reason to avoid it, almost every man will be riveted by porn. Men are visually stimulated, and for a man to walk away or look away from an attractive naked or semi-naked woman is extremely difficult. If other people are around, the personal embarrassment usually will drive them away. But when no one is present, that's when men get into trouble.

Addictive, Progressive, and Destructive

Three factors make porn especially insidious. It is addictive, progressive, and destructive. That means that when a boy or man sees a little, the images stick in his mind and he cannot wait until he can to see more. He stays up late with the computer, unable to turn it off. It feels like an alien force has invaded his body and taken control. He knows every cable channel that will show porn. His obsession is usually very private, behind closed doors, because guys feel slimy about it. If you are around guys who boast of their porn-viewing exploits, you have some serious loser toads on hand. They might have some endearing qualities that initially attracted you, but I guarantee they are relationship disasters.

Many of those Christian guys mentioned in the sex maniac chapter walk into its clutches even though they honestly want to avoid it. Guys who have no moral foundation will be consumed by porn. You won't know about it because most guys would not describe their addiction. They might admit to viewing porn sometimes, but not to the degree of compulsion. Males are too embarrassed by their uncontrollable nature and the fact that masturbation is often a part of the experience. A guy is not going to tell you about this, even if you ask him outright. The humiliation is too great.

The progressive nature of porn is why it moves from embarrassing to dangerous and becomes destructive. Men are constantly looking for more stimulation. Satisfaction is unattainable if a man does not have a spiritual, moral, or ethical belief system. He will be searching constantly for sexual satisfaction but will never truly find it. After awhile, ordinary women performing ordinary sex acts is not stimulating enough so he must see more bizarre acts. The worst of porn combines sex with violence or domination. Eventually, he will have a completely distorted view of what is normal, healthy lovemaking. The makers of porn have no concern for what is genuinely desired or pleasurable for the woman. The movies are made to feed the male quest for more stimulation. Much of it is repugnant, painful, or dangerous for women. Yet, the man watches it, and might expect it from his wife. You do not want to be married to that man. Unfortunately, this type of man is much more common than you think. Being single would be much better than being married to a man like this.

More Problems

Even more problems exist if you marry a guy with porn images locked in his mind. You will keep getting older and wrinkled while his porn stars remain young. You will look bad by comparison. You basically have another woman in the marriage. His sex drive is split between you and the porn. He has less need and desire to woo and romance you because the porn is meeting much of his need. Porn requires no relationship, no commitment, no conversation, no sacrifice, no effort—just self-centered pleasure. Children are never around as part of porn movies or to show the possible results of sex. Porn never nags or asks a man to take out the garbage or accept a shred of responsibility for his actions. It's hard if not impossible for a real, live woman to compete with porn for her husband.

Pornography is a cancer that destroys, leaving in its wake ruined men, exploited women, broken marriages, abused children, disease, crime, and sometimes violent death. For the sake of your future family, you must learn to discern a man's true character. The only good news here is that pornography is a great, definitive toad identification tool. If he is into porn, don't waste another ten seconds on him. Note however, that probably 99–100% of adult males have seen porn in some shape or form. The question is: Do they embrace it or resist it?

That's the real deal on pornography. It's ugly and sad, but you need to know it.

Chapter 52

The Love Test

"How do you know he loves you? How do you know he's yours?"
—Princess Giselle *(Amy Adams)—Enchanted*

AMY ADAMS PONDERED this question in *Enchanted* as she danced through Central Park. She had a number of great suggestions about love but she never covered the ultimate tool to discern the "true love" of a prince. Any woman can administer The Love Test.

The Love Test

Sex can be a powerful tool to define and evaluate a man. You can very quickly screen a lot of toads. The topic of sex could come up in a casual conversation before you ever spend time together or it could be on your fifth wonderful date.

If you are like most women, you are looking for love, not sex. A common question in life is, "How will I know when I am in love?" or "How can I know that he really loves me?" The common romantic movie answers are, "No one can answer that but you," or "You will feel it in your heart," or "You will know by his kiss," or "You will just *know it* when it is right." Those answers are fine for a movie, but in real life, they are worthless.

A test to help you with this question does exist. It can be given at any point in a relationship. It cannot prove that he loves you, but it can positively prove if he does *not* love you.

How to Administer the Test

Perhaps you are in normal conversation or he is making sexual advances or suggestions. You can reveal the following non-negotiable position in a very friendly, matter-of-fact way.

Here is a possible statement you could use, "Yes, sometimes I wonder about sex, especially since I see it in movies and hear about it all the time. I know it must be great, but I have decided to unleash my bottled up sexuality on my husband, whoever the lucky guy turns out to be. I don't want to waste anything on any guy who is not my husband. What do you think about that?" Be sure you ask this in a genuine, friendly manner because you really do want to know what he thinks.

If he loses interest in the relationship, your work is done. You just spared yourself from wasting another minute of your time on a toad. You can cordially close out the date or the conversation. You can be certain that he is a toad if he is not willing to live with that kind of plan. You were simply intended to be his sexual outlet.

Even if you've had prior sexual relationships or you're not sure if you can follow through on the statement, this test question will still weed out a lot of losers.

Any girl who provides sexual favors or intercourse for a guy has given up her most powerful tool for discerning his true character. Since the consequences of a bad marriage are so great, don't you want to be using your most important tool to your advantage? Don't have sex and see what happens. If a guy is truly smitten with you and thinks you may be his future wife, he will be willing to sacrifice his own desires to honor your honorable wishes. Since our culture has embraced sex in typical dating relationships, this approach might be a baffling new concept for him. It will be very difficult for him to change his views, but he might be willing to try. The promise of bottled up sexuality unleashed on a guy for a lifetime is a significant pot of gold at the end of the marriage rainbow if he truly believes you may be the one for him.

Not a Nun

I know you are not a nun. Sexual restraint may be as difficult for you as it is for him. That is why it is so important to have a rational plan that allows you to get to know each other deeply without having sex. The natural progression of a man and woman becoming more emotionally intimate leads to more physical intimacy. It takes a plan made in the daylight if you intend to avoid the natural progression in the dark.

A man who cannot control his sexual urges when he is single is unlikely to control them when he is married. Affairs, pornography, and unreasonable sexual expectations kill a lot of marriages, but those things do not have to kill yours!

The Love Test is described in more detail by Mike Long in *Everybody Is Not Doing It.*

Chapter 53

More Clues about Your Man

FROM THE LOVE TEST

IF THE MAN you are dating expects high physical intimacy or sex at the beginning stage of a relationship, you can know that he has a shallow but common view of the power of sex. You can also assume that he has had other partners if each relationship begins with sexual activity.

Perhaps you are hitting it off quite well and you are both seriously attracted to one another. Maybe you are both thinking this could be the one and you are ready to take it to a higher level. Perhaps you believe that if two adults are mature, committed, in love, and consenting, sex would be the next logical step. Sex would bond you together and allow you to find out if you are compatible physically.

That seems to be the standard line of logic when you have reached an important and risky fork in the road in the progression of your relationship. You can either sleep with him or administer the love test. You are a cautious, reasonable person so you would really like to know how much he loves you *before* you give him your body and some of your soul. Your predicament is that once you sleep with him, you lose the ability to use the love test. Actually, you can give the test any time when you are single, but it is very difficult to get less intimate once you have been fully intimate. Also, the negative consequences discussed in the rest of this book are already in motion. You have unwisely sacrificed most of the benefit of the Love Test.

Remember this important rule of sex: sex enhances strong relationships and creates a wedge in poor relationships. If an unmarried couple are fairly well matched and get along well, they may find that sleeping together draws them closer together as a couple. No surprise. That is why sex was created; however, when the initial thrill starts to wear off or the relationship starts to show some cracks, sex will likely become a dividing point. Sex is either superglue or dynamite. It might take a few days or a few years, but sooner or later you'll discover that all of that time, you were wrapped up with a man who should not be your husband. What did you miss during that time? How will it affect your future marriage? Remember, only 10% of unmarried couples who live together are still together after five years. That is a revealing statistic.

You can wonder about his love, or you can give the love test. If he thinks you might be the wife of his dreams, but he is unwilling to make a significant sacrifice to get you, you would want to question the sincerity of his "I love you" when he suggested it was time to sleep together. Is he willing to temporarily sacrifice his sexual urges?

He has the opportunity to postpone his gratification for a few months or years while the two of you determine if you should be married. He might really love you. If your relationship grows without sex in the mix and the two of you decide to get married, he wins you as the prize, the grand prize. His prize will include your lifetime of devotion, companionship, compassion, respect, trust, and a lifetime of steady, passionate sex with you (whom he cannot resist at the moment) the way it was designed to be—in marriage.

If he is unable to see that that is a good deal for both of you, he is too dense to be your husband. If he understands the value of the trade-off, there is hope for him. If he has a history with sexual baggage, he might have some serious issues to consider or work through, but at least you can both do it without the additional confusion that comes with sleeping together.

Chapter 54

STDs—Do the Math

MANY BOOKS AND health classes have warned you about sexually transmitted diseases (STDs) so I will only give you a brief reminder. A study on teen STD rates was released recently. It generated much discussion in newspapers, on radio, and on television. The study found that 50% of girls 14–19 stated that they are sexually active. Of those girls, 40% were infected with a sexually transmitted disease.[3] Those are horrible odds. Condoms improve the odds, but are not completely effective against all organisms. Oral sex also transmits STDs. Many STDs can recur throughout a person's entire life and some can cause sterility.

The more experience and sex skill a man has, the more likely he has been exposed to an STD while acquiring his skill. Beware of men who claim to be great lovers. It takes knowledge, skill, and practice to become a great lover and they have likely paid a great price to obtain their alleged prowess.

These terrible odds alone should be frightening enough to convince rational people to refrain, but virtually all of those 14–19 year old girls heard the same warnings in health class and chose to believe that they were somehow immune. Add unwanted pregnancy to these statistics and the odds of ending up with a physical situation you won't like look even more overwhelming. Do the math.

Section Four

DON'T SLEEP WITH HIM

How Not

Chapter 55

Now the Hard Part

IF YOU HAVE read the "Why Not" chapter, I hope I have convinced you to refrain from premarital sex and/or reinforced convictions you already had. The hard part is actually following through. Sexual forces are so powerful that many people who committed themselves to wait for marriage, end up in bed anyway. They are confused, surprised, and regretful when this happens. How does it happen? They underestimated the intense power of attraction and overestimated their own willpower. Waiting until you are married is certainly the path less taken and the more difficult path. Following your emotions will almost certainly lead you to failure. You must make many logical decisions that will position you for success. Let's look at some very practical strategies to keep you out of bed.

Sexual forces are so powerful that many people who committed themselves to wait for marriage end up in bed anyway. They underestimated the intense power of attraction and overestimated their own willpower.

Chapter 56

Hug the Wall

WHEN WE PERCEIVE a risk, we take precautions. If we hike a narrow path to the bottom of the Grand Canyon, we will cautiously watch our step and not goof around on the path. If the path narrows to a ledge a couple of feet wide with a straight drop-off, we may find ourself hugging the wall and being extremely cautious. Now consider if the path was the width of a road meandering through a flat, lovely forest. We would sense no danger and could be carefree while we walk. We could explore off the path, run around, or do whatever we like.

If you and your boyfriend have decided to stay out of bed until you are married, you are on a path that looks as pleasant and harmless as the forest trail but actually has risks like the narrow Grand Canyon ledge. A few missteps and you could be over the edge having sex when you never planned on it.

Most people, especially guys, try to move toward sexual activities. You, on the other hand, are purposely planning to delay sex until you are married. Yours is a much tougher challenge. Many well-intentioned but naïve couples approach the physical intimacy of their relationship as carefree as if they were on that forest trail. A more accurate picture would be a path that is flat and safe to walk on but just off the trail, the terrain slopes gently away. The further you stray from the trail, the steeper the slope becomes until it ends

173

at a cliff. Add wet slippery rocks and banana peels and you have a better picture of the risks.

When you make a romantic dinner for your boyfriend, put on a video, and snuggle on the couch alone at his place, you are in high risk territory. Add some fondling and you are on a slippery slope with a banana peel. Many reasonable people think they have the situation under control, but they underestimate the progressive power of sex and they overestimate their own willpower. This section gives you practical strategies to manage your passions and prevent you from sliding off the path. Without some boundaries in your physical relationship, your chances of avoiding sex until you are married become unlikely. You must recognize the real risks of the slippery slope and take the necessary precautions if you really want to wait until you are married.

To convince you of the slippery slope, we can look at a subgroup of our population that, in theory, would agree that you should wait for marriage to have sex. That group is evangelical Christians. Statistics show that ninety-three percent of adults 18–23 who are in romantic relationships are having sex. For conservative Protestants in relationships and active in their faith, it's near eighty percent.[4] Three major reasons might explain why Christians are having sex almost as much as anyone else. 1) They don't know what their God thinks about sex outside of marriage, 2) they don't care what He thinks, or 3) they intend to abstain but accidentally slide into sex.

Option one is unlikely since the Bible is quite clear on the subject. Even non-Christians assume that Christians are not supposed to have sex before they are married. Option two is common with girls who fear that they will not attract and keep a man unless they follow the patterns of most everyone else. This attitude is understandable since sex is such a reliable male attractant. It also affects dating Christian couples who are so overcome by their passion for each other that they choose not to follow what they said they believe. Abandonment of their convictions may also indicate a lack of commitment or a shallow understanding of their faith. Staying true to one's convictions when the going gets tough is a spiritual battle and may be as important for keeping a couple out of bed as the pragmatic suggestions in this book.

The third option brings us back to our Grand Canyon path analogy. This group has every intention of waiting until marriage, but 80 percent of them find themselves having sex anyway. Good intentions without personal limitations and real commitment of both people will probably find them in bed eventually.

Whether your reasons to wait are spiritual, moral, or practical, you had better have a strategy or your chances of success are shaky.

Chapter 57

Simply Irresistible

AS STATED BEFORE, the purpose of sex is to make babies and to help married people stay happy with each other for a lifetime because of the physical pleasure. Taking sex outside of marriage obviously does not change the pleasure factor or the baby factor. In fact, some elements of sex outside of marriage make it seem almost irresistible.

Mountaintop Experience

Unmarried sex may seem like a mountaintop experience at the moment because the negative consequences do not occur until later. Sex, at the moment, is exhilarating. It could be the most exciting thing the couple has experienced. They think they are on top of a mountain, but they are perched on a cliff that could wash out from underneath them at any moment.

Two other factors besides the inherent pleasure of sex contribute to the almost irresistible enticement. I call them the New Stuff Effect and the Off-limits Effect. Basically, people are attracted to things that are new and things that are off-limits. The inherent pleasure of sex along with these two effects work together efficiently to push people over the edge. Even people who never intended to be sexually active find themselves where they never planned to be. These special effects work the same on

17-year-olds in the back seat of a car as they do on married people in an affair. Here's how it happens.

In normal public and private situations, breasts and genitals are untouchable, which isn't just politeness, it is the law. A person could be arrested for touching if it is unwanted. Everyone knows that these are danger zones. Let's say a couple is together on a date or hanging out. They like each other and have done some kissing. At some point, a line is crossed and one of them touches the other's danger zone. Often, it is "accidental" so that neither party has committed to the act. Both people instantly feel a jolt of lightning because the line was crossed. That bolt of lightning was pleasurable, new, and off limits—"the big three."

If neither person objects, the second accidental touch is absolutely obvious to both, which is a major fork in the road. Both people are electrified by the moment awaiting the response of the other. If neither responds negatively, the answer is clear without any words spoken. The couple has indicated to each other that they are willing to move along the pleasure path. Each step of the way gives a higher thrill because each step is new, further out-of-bounds, and more intensely pleasurable. The couple is in the moment's grip.

When people say, "It just happened. We didn't plan this," they are forgetting that a choice was made at each progressive step. Regardless of their moral view of unmarried sex, all three forces would be affecting them. The danger zones of the partner had been off limits until that moment. Access to forbidden areas is why unmarried sex can be thrilling and terrifying at the same time. The terror may not be enough to stop the action, but the steps are predictable. They could progress very quickly if both people have made clear their desire to have sex or it could happen over weeks with very small steps. Either way, the temporary, immediate pleasure is intensified by these two powerful elements of human nature—attraction to new stuff and forbidden activities.

Chapter 58

The One-Way Road of Passion

Eye Contact to Intercourse

OUR CULTURE AND your boyfriend might be putting pressure on you to abandon your plan, but your biggest challenge will be with yourself. Your human biology and natural urges are incredibly powerful. Once you find a guy you really like, your biggest challenge begins. Even if you have fully committed yourself to this plan, carrying it out is very difficult.

The progression of physical intimacy is a one-way street from eye contact to intercourse. It looks something like this.

1. Look—the first time your eyes meet—a flash of electricity.
2. Touch—hand shake, hug, dancing
3. Touch non-sexual areas—Shoulder rub, hand massage
4. Holding hands—frequently touching
5. Light Kiss—a polite or tender kiss
6. Strong Kiss
7. French Kiss
8. Fondling breasts—this is foreplay
9. Fondling/touching/massaging sexual organs—this is foreplay
10. Sexual intercourse

Given two people who like each other and consider themselves a romantic couple, a relationship will naturally move from number 1 to number 10. The important questions are: how fast will it progress and will any steps be skipped? If you get too close too soon, you will bypass some of the exhilarating physical steps but more importantly, you will not have the time needed to build the solid friendship foundation that will be needed to maintain the relationship once the initial thrill wears off.

A One-Way Street

This avenue of pleasure is a one-way street. Once you have experienced a level of physical intimacy, it is very difficult to be satisfied with anything less. The first time you have eye contact with someone to whom you are attracted, you remember it. You go home and tell your roommates about the dreamy guy you met today or you just remember the moment and replay it with pleasure in your mind. It is a quite enjoyable diversion.

If you are attracted to him, the first time you touch will be a bolt of electricity—even if your pinky fingers just touch for a moment. You will remember it and hope for slightly more—perhaps he would touch your back briefly as he guides you through a doorway. Innocent contact that would mean absolutely nothing between people with no attraction becomes powerfully magnified and exciting between people enjoying some attraction—especially if it is mutual attraction. You could describe increased exhilaration of each progressive step.

A healthy relationship savors each step and takes the needed time to grow before progressing to the next level. You must not jump ahead or rush the steps because it is very difficult to reduce the level of physical intimacy. Human nature always strives for more intimacy. Once you have held hands, an incidental brush of your pinky fingers will not generate any sparks. Likewise, if you

> *A healthy relationship savors each step and takes the needed time to grow before progressing to the next level.*

kissed for two seconds today, you will want to kiss for at least three seconds tomorrow. If you have French kissed, a simple light kiss will seem lame; however, if you have not French kissed, the strong kiss will be thrilling. Obviously, sexually active couples will continue to do all ten steps, but the magic of the early steps can only be maximized by taking your time.

Where Is the Line?

If you have decided that you want to save sex for your marriage, you had better understand how you fit into this list. Friendships operate in phases 1, 2, and 3. The moment you move to No. 4 or above, you are a couple to some degree. Somewhere, you must draw a line to limit how far up the list you will go. People who choose not to have sex before marriage would at the least draw the line between 9 and 10. Most people, but not all people, consider kissing to be part of the romantic relationship, so your line would probably be at least between 5 and 6. The further up the list you go, the more intense the pleasure becomes and the more likely you are to hit a point of no return in which it becomes extremely difficult to halt the avalanche of emotional and physical pleasure.

The high risk really begins at the French kiss. Here you start to enter each other's body. Something about this level of intimacy triggers biological responses that stir up the sexual intensity. It is deceiving because most Hollywood kisses are open mouthed, passionate moments. The romantic stars finally get together and the first kiss is a French kiss. So, if the first kiss is a French kiss, you may have sexual arousal very early in a relationship.

What Is Sex?

Many people would argue that anything short of number 10 is not really sex. I would argue that fondling breasts and sex organs is just the early phases of sex. They are foreplay. The purpose of foreplay is to build the level of sexual excitement and response so that both bodies will be ready for intercourse. By human nature, numbers 8 and 9 will sweep a couple right into number 10. If both people genuinely want to avoid intercourse, they might resist for days or weeks, but it is very unlikely that a couple could engage in heavy petting sessions repeatedly and not eventually move all the way to intercourse.

The problem is that once any line is crossed even once from a low number to a higher number, people automatically desire to get back to the highest point of excitement; therefore, to discontinue a routine of heavy petting is difficult. Backing up one more step, the French kiss can easily begin sexual arousal and take you to the brink of foreplay. It is all a slippery slope. The slope starts out very gradually with innocent kisses and then shifts to a very steep slide. Obviously you will not be shaking hands with your boyfriend to say good night; however, you and your boyfriend must understand the importance of setting limits on physical intimacy and both commit to not violating the limits you set.

Chapter 59

It's Just a Matter of Time

ACCORDING TO THE book, *Too Close Too Soon: Avoiding the Heartache of Premature Intimacy* by Dr. Jim Talley and Dr. Bobbie Reed, intercourse is only a matter of time. By the time a couple has spent about 300 hours together, they will very likely be to the point of intercourse. It generally takes that much time for a couple to get to know each other well. Obviously, 300 hours is a huge generalization, but it seems close to accurate from what I have experienced and observed. This timeframe refers to a couple who intends to wait until they are married for their first sex. For a couple without that conviction, they could go from number 1 to number 10 in two hours. In that case, the relationship is virtually doomed from the start. People willing to move that fast have serious self-esteem issues that would make a healthy relationship quite difficult. Couples who rush to sex bypass the essential steps required to build a solid, durable relationship. Like a fine wine, vintage relationships cannot be rushed.

The 300-hour timeline helps explain why it is so difficult for couples to endure a three-year engagement if they also intend not to have sex before marriage. If they build a solid foundation for the relationship, the couple becomes more intimate spiritually and in their knowledge of one another's shared emotions, thoughts, and dreams. All of these forms of intimacy are important and healthy. The ironic twist is that physical intimacy will want to follow along. The more you give your heart to your man, the more you will long to give him your body too. Once again, these natural urges are another reason you must make very specific decisions if you honestly want to succeed in saving sex for marriage for all the reasons in the "Don't Have Sex with Him—Why Not" section.

Chapter 60

The Red Zone

IN FOOTBALL, THE area between the 20-yard line and the end zone is called the red zone. When a team enters the red zone, both teams and the fans get excited because they anticipate that something is about to happen. The offense might score or the defense might make a stand and prevent a touchdown that seemed imminent. The game is most intense in the red zone.

When dating, there are circumstances and activities that can easily put you into the red zone. The relational red zone describes circumstances when you are at an increased likelihood of becoming sexually intimate. There is certainly nothing wrong with these red zone settings. I am not suggesting that you must avoid these factors; however, you should know that as you combine risk factors, your chances of sexual intimacy increase.

Red Zone Indicators

Darkness
Evening
Assured privacy
No plan—just hanging out
Horizontal body position i.e. lying down together
Romantic setting

Extended time together (weekend/vacation)

Like Night and Day

Darkness changes everything. The moon is romantic. The lights of Times Square at night energize the crowds. Few people will dance on a well-lit dance floor; for some reason, the lights must be dimmed. Parties are more exciting at night. People get sleepy at night and think about bed. Night seems to intensify many experiences. It intensifies a date and the emotions that come with the date.

Daylight, on the other hand, lessens the intensity of an experience. Daylight is more everyday and ordinary. Daylight allows you to see everything as it is—good and bad. A daytime date is inherently less romantic and less intense, but it can still be pleasant, fun, and relaxed. Daylight removes some of the pressure to be pretty and smooth. There is less performance expectancy and more inclination to be yourself. Getting dressed up and going out on the town in the evening may be more exciting for many people, but a sweatshirt and pony tail at home might be the time you feel like you are truly being yourself. I do not know why there is such a distinct difference between night and day, but there is.

Assured Privacy

The roommates are gone for the weekend. The parents are out of town. You live alone. If you are alone with your date with total assurance that no one will walk in on you, you will feel total freedom to become more intimate. It would certainly be embarrassing to have someone walk in on you, but assured privacy removes those fears.

The possibility of unexpected company nags at the back of your mind. Part of you might want to move into more intimate contact, but the fear of sudden company can help motivate you to show restraint.

Horizontal vs. Vertical

The fact that sitting on a couch is less intimate than lying on a couch is obvious to anyone. When you are snuggled on a couch, semi-reclining while watching a movie and you shift your positions to become more horizontal, you are moving another step closer to the edge.

Romance vs. Ordinary

Enjoying a romantic meal with candles and soft music is a wonderful experience. I highly recommend it. Most women love and crave romance. If you are with a really special guy and romance is in the air, remember that your crockpot which is normally under your full control might be turned on. Intimacy will probably seem like the next logical step. Your emotions may start to overwhelm your original intentions of avoiding sexual activity.

Extended Time vs. Brief Time

When couples spend extended time together, such as enjoying a long weekend or vacation together, the relationship is more likely to accelerate. In these settings, you will start to feel and act more like a married couple. If you intend *not* to sleep together, you need time to cool down from the excitement of being with the great guy. When you say goodbye from a single date and go back to your own world, you have the time and privacy to rationally process the state of the relationship, cool your romantic passions, and recharge your batteries of resistance needed to overcome your desire to become more physically intimate.

Vacations are intended to disconnect us from the harsh realities of our everyday life. Usually vacations mean relaxation, few responsibilities, good food, pleasant activities, naps, and more. They're great but they're not real life. Vacations or getaways can put us into a temporary, artificial haze of happiness. When shared with a romantic guy, your good judgment becomes impaired. I have several Hawaiian shirts hanging in my closet that seemed like perfect fashion while we were on vacation, but back at home, they are always out of place except at Hawaiian parties. They seemed like a good idea at the time. Extended time is more likely to leave you questioning, "What was I thinking?" when you return to your own home and reconsider your time together.

Yellow Zone

Football has no yellow zone, but I have created one to complete this word picture. Indicators of a yellow dating zone would be daylight, public places, possible unexpected company, sitting or standing, non-romantic activities, and having extra people around. These indicators can add a measure of safety to the time you spend with your special guy. You can use these factors to help control the passion (yours and his) as your relationship grows. I understand that this directly contradicts our natural desire to be very alone and very romantic as a relationship grows. All of your natural desires, if followed, will take you to sexual intimacy if you like each other and spend enough time together. Only your commitment to your higher calling for a happy marriage will keep you out of bed.

Chapter 61

Who Plugged in My Crockpot?

MEN ARE WELL aware of their strong physical urges because they occur so frequently and quickly. (Remember, men are like microwave ovens.) Many women, however, are caught by surprise by the power of their own physical urges when the man or the moment is exceptionally special. The woman did not even know her crockpot was plugged in and suddenly she feels the intense heat.

In dating and relationships, knowing your crockpot nature is critical. Your "on" switch might be activated, and you didn't even realize it. Let's say, for instance, that your man picked you up looking more handsome than you had ever seen him. His heart skipped a beat when he saw you and so did yours. He was a perfect gentleman all evening, treating you like a queen and you are thinking, "I really like this guy." Perhaps you have always had your emotions and actions under control during dating situations. You must beware that your self-control will become more difficult the more you like the guy. When all of the romantic elements line up, you suddenly may find yourself in unfamiliar emotional territory. The combination of emotional, hormonal, and physical responses can be surprisingly powerful, leaving you sizzling when you did not expect it and wondering who plugged in the crockpot.

Chapter 62

"Does Somebody Need a Hug?"

WILL FARRELL, *ELF*

You Need a Hug

EVERY GIRL NEEDS hugs. Girls need to know they are okay. They crave physical touch. They need to be loved. Hugs and affirmation are a virtual necessity for a girl growing up. In a perfect world, she would get this affirmation and affirmative hugs from her father. He is the man who should be protecting her and helping her grow into a young lady, reminding her all the time how much he loves her and how pretty she is inside and out. Physically, she needs regular doses of bear hugs from Dad. If a girl doesn't get her hugs and pure love from her father, she will often seek it somewhere else.

Your need for hugs is important to consider if you are growing up without a dad or your dad does not provide the love, hugs, and support you need. You likely feel a longing to be hugged and appreciated. This is quite real and important. If you have a reasonable relationship with your father, you might want to discuss this with him. Most dads will be thrilled to be able to give you hugs. Sometimes, we dads don't know what to say but we long to be close to our daughters. The chance to provide security and affection to our daughter who is growing up so quickly is a job that most dads would cherish. If there are issues with your father that would prevent this type of relationship, perhaps you could find another trusted adult who could give you a hug when you need it.

191

Regardless of what you do, remember that this thirst for normal affection could drive you to become too intimate with a guy just to meet this need. It always helps to know yourself well.

(I think I will go find one of my daughters to hug.)

Chapter 63

Civilized Women

WOMEN ARE NATURALLY more civilized than men when it comes to relationships. If left to their natural inclinations, most women would get to know a guy pretty well before getting physically intimate. Women's desire for physical intimacy flows from attraction and emotional intimacy which is a healthy and natural progression.

Our culture, however, has successfully shifted the woman to a willingness to be physical before any true friendship or genuine emotional intimacy has had a chance to grow. Many people expect to get acquainted and move straight to physical intimacy. Women have allowed the rush to physical intimacy to happen but it doesn't really make sense to most women. You probably have no interest in kissing some guy you don't even know. A reasonable woman assumes that she would only kiss someone she likes. A woman, by nature, will first give herself emotionally to the man. Only after she is emotionally tied to him is she really comfortable responding physically. The problem is that men are anxious to get to physical pleasure as soon as possible. This causes the woman to mistakenly assume that the guy is already emotionally attached to her. Emotional attachment is a critical element for the woman, but it is strictly optional for the man.

Good Instinct

It is important to understand this phase of the relationship puzzle because you must understand yourself to keep yourself out of bed. In the early phase of a relationship, your instinct and intuition are working in your favor. Rational, sensible, instinctive feminine behavior would have you feel some sort of emotional attachment and commitment with a man before you would sleep with him and probably before you would even start to get physical. Society and males have effectively persuaded women to get physical very early in a relationship, but true female intuition would want some commitment first. So, up to this point, your inner voice is probably giving you good advice unless you have been completely brainwashed by our culture. I'm sure you do not want to kiss just any guy. He must be worthy of your kiss.

Bad Instinct—You Are Your Worst Enemy

Beware, once you get deeper into a relationship, your instinct and intuition will betray you. This phase is entirely different from the early phase. As you become emotionally attached to a guy whom you might genuinely love, everything changes. If you follow your instincts now, you will make huge mistakes. Your feelings and emotions will urge you to give more of yourself. The more you give your heart to him, the more you will want to give of yourself physically. At this point, pressure from your boyfriend or the culture is no longer required; the most intense pressure will come from within yourself. You may genuinely yearn for him. Your own intense emotions will place you in uncharted territory because you have never felt this way before. You have never been with a man this great. You can see it in the movies, read romance novels, and daydream all you want, but the immediate emotional intensity of falling in love is euphoric and powerful. As you fall in love, your natural desire to please him and be more physically intimate will automatically grow. You must have a rational plan, boundaries, and commitment if you wish to counteract the otherwise inevitable progression toward sex.

These two relational phases are radically different and require distinctly different strategies if you want to stay out of bed before you are married in order to enjoy your time in bed more when you are married.

Section Five

DON'T PANIC

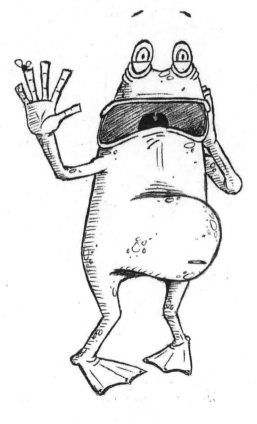

Chapter 64

Here's the Panic Button. Don't Push It

BELOW ARE SOME various situations that can drive a woman to push the panic button. It happens when you become so fearful that you will not find a man that you abandon your relatively sane philosophy and start living in the high risk, high pain, slim chances lane of life.

- A woman leaving college without a man
- A woman in the working world who has no prospects
- A ninth grade girl seeing "all" the other girls with boyfriends and she has no boys interested in her
- A girl in high school about to graduate who has never been asked out or pursued
- A divorcee who is excruciatingly lonely and petrified by the thought of dating again
- A single woman hearing her baby-bearing clock ticking and no men are in sight

These scenarios can be very difficult to face. Be sure you know what your purpose and goals in life are. Review with your best friend if there are things you could do to improve your attractiveness. Consider your conversation, hairstyle, interests, activities, makeup, etc. Do what you can do. Determine that you are going to have a great life with or without a man, then start living that way. If you are still depressed, find more resources at FindingYourPrince.com.

Chapter 65

Never Buy a Swimsuit at a Hardware Store

THE CHANCES OF finding a swimsuit at a hardware store are poor. If you were to stumble upon a Home Depot with swimsuits, not only would that be odd, but your selection would probably not be as good as if you were shopping at Old Navy or your favorite swimsuit retailer. Your shopping instincts would never take you to Home Depot to find a swimsuit.

If you hope to find a prince, your chances of finding one at a bar or club are about the same as those of finding a swimsuit at a hardware store. Why? Because clubs are stocked with toads. If a prince happens to be there, how would you pick him out from the rest of the crowd? They all look alike and you have no way to differentiate. If "good dancer" was on your list of husband qualities, you had better cross it off. Change it to "willing to learn to dance," and you are in better territory. Most of the happiest marriages I know include a man who is a pathetic dancer. Likewise, a great dancer could be a great guy. So, dancing talent and party skills are irrelevant in the prince hunt. If you love music, dancing, and parties, that's great, but don't fool yourself into thinking that you will find a good man at the club.

Many intelligent single women build their social life around clubbing and parties. Their swimsuit intuition reliably leads them away from the hardware store, but their princely intuition has let them down as they waste night after night at clubs where they have virtually no chance of finding a quality man. Toads, however, are in abundant supply.

Ruth and I love to dance. We watch people leave weddings early and think about all the fun they are missing. We were recently at a wedding, and I was reminded of my college days at parties and bars. These locations are environments carefully designed to make communication challenging. As soon as the music cranks up, conversation is reduced to short phrases yelled over the music. Lots of leaning in closer to yell your comment a second time takes place. It's particularly tough to talk if you like to inject wit or nuances into your comments. There is nothing nuanced about screaming your witty line a second time. You end up doing lots of smiling and nodding.

When you give up on talking, you can head to the dance floor. Depending on the place, the dancing could range from basic wedding dancing to people virtually having sex on the dance floor. Either way, while dancing, you learn nothing more about the other person, but at least you don't have to yell any more. If you are unable to learn anything significant about the people at a club, you are reduced to picking guys at random or responding to guys who approach you based entirely on your looks or danceability. It could take you a very long time to stumble upon a prince using random selection at a club.

How bizarre that clubs are the primary hunting ground for so many people. The routine for many singles is to head out every weekend for a club. Young women in their prime squander their time this way and radically reduce their chances of finding a quality guy. It's so irrational. Parties, clubs, and bars are not necessarily bad, but they are terrible for spouse shopping. So if you like to dance and mingle periodically, that's fine, but don't expect to find your prince there.

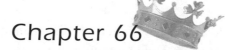

Chapter 66

Where Are the Princes Hiding?

SO, YOU WONDER, where does a girl meet a potential prince? There is no magic formula. Participating in activities that are interesting or meaningful will increase the chances that you will run into a like-minded guy. However, doing an activity as a man hunt is not a good idea. This puts pressure on the activity and might make you feel desperate. With that said, here is a list of ways to meet new and interesting people and hopefully, make some genuine friendships—male or female.

Ways to meet new people

1. Join a club that does something you enjoy or involves an activity you want to explore.
2. Volunteer somewhere. Besides helping with a worthy cause, volunteering helps you network with many people who might eventually connect you with a quality guy.
3. Join a book club and discuss something interesting.
4. Play a coed sport.
5. Work with a river clean-up project or other environmental service.

6. Build a house with Habitat for Humanity. The company can use anyone, and you will be taught which end of the hammer to hold or you will be given other helpful duties.
7. Go to church. Get involved in serving someone or participate in a small group Bible study. You must get into activities that allow you to really get to know people. Otherwise, you can attend for a long time and still feel disconnected. Many churches also have activities specifically for single people.
8. Work the phones at PBS or a local charity.
9. Work on a political campaign.
10. Attend a self-improvement workshop.
11. Do a bike-a-thon, walkathon, or a charity bike tour.
12. Attend a convention of interest.
13. Join or organize a supper club.
14. Take swing dance or ballroom dance lessons.
15. Go to a contradance. You do not need to know how to dance and do not need a partner. Usually it is a friendly crowd. Contradances can be like a square dance or the dancing in *Pride and Prejudice*.

You want to avoid spending too much time at home wishing you were out. Home is fine if that is where you want to be. But a giant bowl of Moose Tracks ice cream sprinkled with self-pity is not a balanced meal. Do not entertain yourself to death watching movies and TV. It's depressing to watch everyone else enjoy life on the screen while you watch from your couch. You will improve your self-esteem by actively doing things rather than being passive. Serving or helping others is one of the most reliable ways to fight loneliness. The focus is removed from your own situation and your self-esteem experiences a surprisingly powerful boost.

Consider inviting a girlfriend to join you in an activity. However, be sure to extend friendship to others in the group. You'll be tempted to hide behind the security of the person you already know, especially if you're shy or insecure, but remember that one of the reasons you are there is to meet new people. Also consider inviting someone you do not know well and you might become good friends.

Chapter 67

No Need to Get Married

PERHAPS EVERY CELL in your body is screaming that you want to be married or maybe just a few cells are murmuring. In any case, men must not hear even a whisper of desperation in your words or actions. Guys are frightened off if they sense desperation because they are afraid you will get too serious too fast. And remember that blatant flirtation is a sign of desperation. You also lose some of your appeal if you behave as though you have been overlooked.

How do you camouflage your true feelings? The best way is to actually change your attitude. You are not a slave to your current attitude; you can change it any time you want. If you are looking for a new attitude, I would like to suggest this one. Begin to tell yourself, "I would probably like to get married some day, but I will be perfectly content with my life if marriage

A recommended attitude for you to adopt: "I would probably like to get married some day, but I will be perfectly content with my life if marriage doesn't happen. For now I want to make the most of each day, enjoying the things I can do while I am single."

doesn't happen. For now I want to make the most of each day, enjoying the things I can do while I am single." If you can adopt this attitude or something like it, you will be in a much better position to put into action the other suggestions in this book that will increase your chances of finding your prince.

There are many exciting things you can do when you are single that are much more difficult if you are married, such as getting a college degree, traveling, and pursuing your interests. The chances are fairly good that you will end up married; therefore, make the most of your single years, assuming they could end at any time. The last thing you want to do is feel sorry for yourself because you don't have your soul mate yet. That attitude will cause you to waste some of your best years. The more you grab life by the horns and live to the fullest, the more likely it will be that you will come upon a like-minded man. As Horace, the great Roman poet said, "Seize the day!"

Chapter 68

The Disease: Low Self-Esteem The Cure: A Boyfriend

GIRLS NATURALLY HAVE low self-esteem. A study done a few years ago to find the most serious issues with which women struggle found the number one issue to be low self-esteem.

While guys tend to think too much of themselves, girls tend to think too little of themselves. Girls worry that they are not smart enough, not pretty enough, too fat, too thin, too tall, or too short. They think their eyes are too big, their hair is too straight or too curly, they're not very popular, and the list goes on. Very few girls escape this way of thinking which all stems from low self-esteem. The general feeling is, "I am not worthwhile and I'll always fall short."

Women have a sure-fire yet deceptive cure for low self-esteem; a boyfriend. If a boy is willing to call you his girlfriend, you must be okay; therefore, the hunt is on for the boy who will cure your low self-esteem problem. Many men and boys understand your situation and know exactly what to say and do to prey on this weakness.

The Typical Spiral

When a boy is finally interested in a girl, she starts seeing him and soon she's floating on air with happiness. The more she is with him, the more she likes him, and the more she gives her heart to him. The more she gives of her heart, the more she wants to give to him physically. Eventually, sexual activity and intercourse occur. The chase is over and so is his interest in her so he breaks it off. She is so devastated that her self-esteem drops to an even lower level than before she had the boyfriend in the first place. She is so desperate to feel relief that she will do almost anything to find a cure; i.e. a new boyfriend. She has experience now and knows exactly how to get a boy's attention. Even though it's a hollow "love," before long, she has a new boyfriend. They spend time together, she likes him, they proceed to physical intimacy, and the relationship dies. The cycle continues—a downward spiral of heartache and despair. Her baggage is packed and she carries it to each succeeding relationship.

High school, college, thirty-something—the age doesn't matter. Cycle lengths and frequency will vary. Someone could live with a guy for two days or two years and will experience the same parts of the cycle.

Chapter 69

Loneliness and Sex

TWO OF THE most powerful motivational forces in the universe are the fear of loneliness and the sex drive. These two forces are so influential, they steer many of us to do things that don't make much sense. You might be suffering from excruciating loneliness at this very moment. Many people display a brave exterior to the world while they are melting on the inside. The thought of a lifetime of that pain can seem unbearable. Many times sex and loneliness are the controlling factors in relational decisions. What an irony that our brains get hijacked by these two powerhouses at the very time we are making decisions that can affect us for a lifetime.

I recently had a conversation with a fellow veterinarian who was surprised by a divorce several years ago. She is a very articulate, intelligent, enjoyable person to be around. She has a DVM and a PhD, has supervised large groups of professionals, and has the rare combination of technical expertise combined with excellent people skills. She described the excruciating loneliness she feels, especially after her recent boyfriend of 12 months decided to move on. She has many regrets about her decisions and behavior after the divorce, particularly sleeping with men she did not know very well. Her life has been turned upside down because she found herself willing to do anything to relieve the loneliness. Although she is one of the most thoughtful, rational people I know, she made a series of completely irrational decisions when it came to this critical part of her life. There is no correlation among education, social status, and relationship wisdom. People who make great decisions in every other aspect of life can easily veer off course in their romantic lives.

It Makes No Sense but It Happens All the Time

It's frustrating and confusing when we hear about women who are in an abusive relationship but refuse to walk away from it. How could a woman possibly keep returning to a man who beats her or emotionally abuses her? One answer is the fear of loneliness. The fear of being alone in the world is great enough to drive her back into her nightmare. Her desperate choices demonstrate the depth of fear.

If you know it's wrong for a woman to stay in an emotionally or mentally abusive relationship and you are in one, stop abusing yourself and get out. You may think that you would never stay in an abusive relationship and I hope you are right; however, you might be tempted to stay with a mediocre guy. Perhaps he has some qualities that are endearing, but he certainly is not really what you had hoped for in a boyfriend or husband. Yet, your fear of being alone can overwhelm your normal good judgment and cause you to stay with him.

"Anyone is better than no one" is not a recommended philosophy when it comes to picking boyfriends who might become husbands. Set your standards high. Don't settle for someone you can just tolerate. At the same time, remember that Mr. Perfect does not exist. It's an important judgment call every girl must make. Be sure you are thinking as clearly as possible as you make this judgment. Nothing muddles the mind quicker than adding sex to the mix.

> "A large majority of female divorcees say that their married years were the loneliest years of their lives."
>
> —Stoeker and Arterburn, *Every Woman's Desire*

Do not think that a boyfriend will automatically relieve the pain of your loneliness. If you are not well matched or have a shallow foundation to your relationship, you can easily find yourself even lonelier than you are now when the relationship unravels, especially if you are married when it unravels. It is important to soothe your loneliness with good solid friendships with either gender that will provide the inner support you need. With this support, you will feel less compulsion to find a boyfriend to relieve the pain of loneliness. If you find a boyfriend, that's great; but you do not want to live your life with a desperate need for male companionship.

Chapter 70

Desperate Times, Desperate Actions

FEAR AND DESPERATION can make people do amazing things. We have a family story about my grandfather who heaved a huge safe out of a second story window when his house caught on fire. I grew up with that safe in our basement. As a boy, I could not move it an inch. As a man, I can scooch it a little but certainly could not lift it. Yet, when my grandfather was frightened and desperate, he tossed it out the window by himself. People eat worms and drink urine in survival situations. One man amputated his own arm when it was crushed under a boulder trapping him alone in a mountainous region where he would have died. Yikes! It is hard to imagine these amazing actions in the middle of an ordinary comfortable day, but desperation and fear are amazing motivators.

If you fear that you will never attract a man and are feeling desperate about your situation, you are positioned to do things that you would not consider in the course of your ordinary life. Women will go to risky places and do risky things to attract a guy. Let's assume you have found a man and started a reasonable relationship. Eventually, it seems serious and you decide to sleep together. You have a good fish on the line and feel desperate to get the fish in the boat. You like him a lot and hope you will get married. You are desperate to impress him. You are also loaded with fears of inadequacy regarding your appearance and performance. You are certainly not in an emotionally safe environment. If you do not measure up in any of these areas, he may walk. So your fear and desperation lead you to do whatever he wants and then some. You may do things that you do not enjoy or that you find repugnant or demeaning. He, on the other hand, may be thrilled with your performance. More of this kind of pleasure looks very appealing to the man.

The big question you must answer is: How long do you plan to keep this amazing performance going? You might be able to do it long enough to get him married. Then what? Shortly into the marriage, you break the news to him that you never really enjoyed that activity, and you will not be doing it any longer, which, I can assure you, is not a great start for a lifetime together. Men do not like to backtrack on the intensity of their pleasure.

Unintended consequences can sneak up on you and slam you when it is too late. Many people do not anticipate the potential trap they may set for themselves in the future. Don't think that I am advocating premarital sex as long as you don't get crazy. All of the negative consequences remain for any form of sex before marriage. If you feel desperate to have a man, beware that desperation can be dangerous.

Chapter 71

All Women Agree, But …

"NO GIRL OR woman should ever be forced to do something sexually that she does not want to do."

This statement is not only true, but it is backed up by the law. The statement could be expanded to read, "No woman should be forced, coerced, teased, demeaned, bullied, blackmailed, manipulated, or tricked into doing anything sexually that she does not want to do." The rest of this book may be controversial, but this statement should be universally embraced by all women.

A recent study found that 40 percent of girls between 14–22 years of age had experienced non-consenting sex acts. Another study showed 40 percent of girls interviewed said that, on at least one occasion, they had sex when they didn't want to. Ten percent said that their boyfriends forced them to have sex.[5] A study from Britain's Bristol University reports that one in three teenage girls had suffered sexual abuse from a boyfriend and one in four experienced violence in a relationship. One in six girls had been pressured into having sex and one of every sixteen claimed to have been raped.

All women would agree violence and coercion should not be tolerated, yet naïve and insecure women continually allow themselves to be pressured into sex acts they do not want to do or stay with a guy who has already abused them in some way. Any man you are dating who strikes you or threatens you in any way should be dropped immediately. There is nothing more to discuss no matter how much he begs. Walk away and stay away.

Exploitation in Thailand and the US

In places like Thailand, young children are sold into sex rings. They are slaves to be raped and sexually abused every day of their lives. Now, in the USA, we see our own children as young as 11 or 12 years old are having oral sex parties. More than fifty percent of youth (ages 15–19) have had oral sex.[6] Both Thailand and the US are exploiting children. Americans are just doing it indirectly. Our young girls are being exploited by our own culture that has convinced them that sexual favors are expected if you want to attract a boy. The sad reality is that many adult women are just as brainwashed as the 7th grade girls. If adults do not understand the seriousness of oral sex, how can we teach our children self-respect?

Hot Potato

One sex act that may involve coercion is oral sex. Oral sex is a controversial and delicate subject. In our marriage counseling, we do not say yea or nay. It is certainly a form of sex. Many women consider it repugnant or undesirable, yet we do not consider it taboo in our counseling. Married couples have tremendous freedom to explore how to give each other pleasure; however, the first sentence of this chapter is the critical safety net that allows married couples creative freedom to explore their sexuality without hurting each other.

Women especially need this protection—that is the right to say no. The difference is like the decision between walking a tight rope with a safety net under you or walking the tightrope over Niagara Falls without one. The safety net (the right to say no) is absolutely essential for every single and married woman of any age. In order for it to work, you must know of it and promise yourself now to use it if you need it. Never give in if you are pressured to do something you do not want to do.

Manipulation 101

Many guys might consider oral sex to be as good as or even better than intercourse. No risk of pregnancy exists, the physical pleasure is similar to intercourse, and the male can be 100% self-centered. He does not think of the girl for even a moment. He will obviously tell her how wonderful she is. Every toad knows to say that from Manipulation 101 because he wants this to happen again. Another manipulation technique is for the guy to make some innocent-sounding bet over a card game or a piece of trivia. The loser will do whatever the other says. When the girl is asked to pay up with a sexual favor, she is caught between breaking her word and doing something she does not want to do. Games like Truth or Dare can land you in the same position.

Some guys use it as a negotiation tool. When they are turned down for intercourse, they offer oral sex as a compromise, claiming that it is not really having sex. Naive girls buy it. Many of the consequences are the same as intercourse. Sexually transmitted diseases can be picked up. The esteem of the guy goes up and the esteem of the girl goes down because she has allowed herself to be used.

Bragging Rights

You must know that it is virtually impossible for a guy to remain silent over this accomplishment. He has successfully convinced a girl to provide this service for nothing. He might consider this conquest the most important achievement of his life. By the next day or on the day of your breakup, he will be advertising your services to the rest of the male community. He may not seem like the type at the moment. You saw something appealing about him when you agreed to go out. Yet, he only needs to tell one guy. That guy has a hot story and has no reason to protect your reputation so the news makes its way around. You may never hear it. You are not around for this male toad talk, but I can assure you that it is happening.

Prostitutes around the country offer this service for $50+ per session. What are you worth?

Your New Big Problem

Now you need to worry about the motives of the next boy who seems interested in you. Exactly why is he interested? Is he interested in you or in your reputation? You have no way of knowing. This scenario especially applies to communities of people such as school, college, workplace, neighborhood, etc. Good reputations can be lost in a single day, yet bad ones can last a lifetime.

This same chain of events can take place with intercourse as well. It is a dangerous world, and you are playing with live ammunition. You have a genuine, healthy, normal craving to be loved by someone, but a single misstep can take you to places you never wanted to be. If you have done things that you regret, the greatest tragedy would be if you continue to allow yourself to be manipulated.

If you have not made these mistakes, you can be thankful and resolve not to be taken in by the ruse. The guy who pressures you for sexual favors has little to lose. You are the only one who lives with the consequences of your decisions.

Most faiths, including Christianity, consider oral sex to be an actual form of sex and put it right alongside intercourse in their teaching. If intercourse is wrong outside of marriage, then so is oral sex. Some clever Christian singles think they have outsmarted God with a loophole that would allow them to engage in oral sex freely because it is not intercourse. They "caught God on a technicality." Of course, if you don't care what God thinks, this wouldn't influence your decision. If you do believe in God, consider that He makes rules to protect people, not to make them miserable.

Oral Sex Facts

A number of studies have demonstrated that oral sex is not necessarily safe. Both giving and receiving oral sex can lead to the transmission of sexually transmitted diseases. The most common STD transmitted via oral sex is herpes. Herpes causes cold sores around the mouth or genital sores. Genital sores can be transmitted to the mouth and mouth sores can be transmitted to genitals.

The human papilloma virus causes genital warts and can also very occasionally be transmitted through oral sex. HPV can cause warts to appear around or inside the mouth a woman who has given oral sex to an infected man.

Gonorrhea has been shown to infect the throat of some people who have given oral sex to an infected person. This infection can then be passed on from the throat to the genitals of any future partners. Chlamydia can also infect the throat in a similar way, although this is less common. Both infections may result in a sore throat, although many people will remain asymptomatic and unaware they are infected.

Syphilis may be passed on during oral sex if a person's mouth comes into contact with an open sore or a skin rash caused by the infection.[7]

Recently, an increase in oral cancers has been linked to an increase in oral sex. Oral sex is not safe sex.

> ... even as parents obsessively strap bike helmets on their kids'
> heads and squirt antiseptic gels on their hands,
> the adults themselves cavalierly break up families with divorce and
> tolerate the rampant sexualization of prepubescent girls.
> In short, we're focusing on the wrong *risks*.
>
> —Hara Marano, *Nation of Wimps*

Section Six

RATIONAL RELATIONSHIPS

Chapter 72

Here's a Quarter, Call Someone Who Cares

TRAVIS TRITT

SOMETIMES OUR JUDGMENT becomes blurred when we think we are in love. Fortunately our friends and family are probably still seeing clearly. Before becoming seriously attached to a guy, you can get some great insight by asking the people who know you best what they think of him. This can be done anytime in a friendship or relationship but should always be done before anybody gets married. Hopefully, you will hear warm fuzzies about how great a guy he is and you'll hear the truth about his character strengths and weaknesses.

Before you ask for an opinion, you should understand some of the psychology at work. Many people do not like to give their opinion unless someone asks for it. Interestingly, most people love to voice their opinion to anyone other than the involved person. If you want to know what a trusted friend or family member thinks of your fiancé, you will probably need to ask her directly. That person must understand that you truly want an honest answer. Otherwise, she may just tell you, "Sure, I think he's great."

If you get that answer, follow up with, "What are his three biggest strengths as husband material?" This gives your friend a chance to say something nice about him. If you get an awkward silence, you are in trouble. Most of his good points, you probably already know.

Then ask the important question. "What are three things that might be trouble spots or might make him hard to live with?" You may have to reassure your friend that you would never tell the guy and you will not hold it against her if you do decide to marry him.

This type of honest exchange can only be done between people who trust each other completely. You must be open-minded and teachable, then you can make an informed choice. Beware of getting defensive over any criticism. It may be scary for your friends to say what they honestly think, but they are speaking out of love for you, not out of condemnation of your guy.

I'm Not Gonna Tell Him!

I have watched several friends and family members get married to people who I thought would be trouble. On one occasion, I remember sitting around with friends discussing how much we disliked the wife-to-be and asking what on earth he saw in her. (I will not divulge the identity no matter how long you torture me. Gender in this story may have been changed to protect my future.) Joking and humorous predictions about their life together ensued.

"Are you gonna tell him?"

"I'm not going to tell him. I think *you* should do it."

"I'm not going to do it."

Nobody did it. He got married and divorced three years later. No one was laughing during the divorce.

"I knew she was no good."

We all knew, but no one had the courage to confront him; after all, he might not have listened anyway. Of the other couples I have worried about, some have divorced, some are still together with struggles, and some are doing fine. In all of these cases, I did not have the backbone to challenge them on their choice of spouse. I do not like to butt into people's lives uninvited.

The problem is that no one thinks they are the right person to question your choice of spouse. Casual friends don't know him well enough. Good friends don't want to harm the friendship. Family members do not want to be known as "the father-in-law (sister, cousin, etc.) who never liked the guy from the start." It is quite awkward if the new spouse knows that the father suggested that they not get married. Parents know this and hold their tongues unless the guy is an absolute monster. Most parents will make a strong effort to welcome a new son-in-law into the family even if they do not fully approve of the marriage. They want their daughter to be happy.

Perhaps the Most Important Advice of Your Life

In order to overcome any reluctance to speak truthfully, you must directly ask for insight from the people you trust the most. These people will recognize the seriousness of the question and offer carefully considered thoughts. No one is perfect and you might choose to marry your guy even though he received some poor reviews. Getting these evaluations at least gives you a chance to carefully consider if you can live with the flaws that your friends and family members might point out. You are getting off on the right foot by being sure you can love him as he is and not desiring to change him into what makes you happy.

If the people who love you the most think you are a great match, this reassuring stamp of approval can help you proceed with confidence and joy. There's great wisdom in seeking advice or insight for the most important decision of your life, especially when your mind is slightly mushy from being in love.

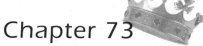

Chapter 73

Everybody Needs Counseling

EVERY COUPLE CONSIDERING marriage needs counseling. Even the most perfectly-matched couple will benefit from meeting with a counselor to help prepare for marriage and to make sure both people really know what they are in for. Many churches provide counseling services for free or low cost. Counselors can provide compatibility tests that act as a great start to identify possible stresses before you say "I do." Most people find it enjoyable to talk through real issues of life with the one they love and good counselors will help facilitate constructive and revealing discussions. Topics may include money, sex, love, in-laws, vacations, child rearing, anger issues, control, difficult family situations, communication skills, religion, and many more.

A book you might find helpful before or after you are engaged is *101 Questions to Ask Before You Get Engaged* by Norman Wright. Another source of premarital counseling is the PREP program. PREP (Prevention and Relationship Enhancement Program) is one of the most comprehensive and well respected divorce-prevention/marriage-enhancing programs in the world. PREP is a skills and principles-building curriculum designed to help partners say what they need to say, get to the heart of problems, and increase their connection with each other. Go to http://www.prepinc.com for more information.

Chapter 74

Whatever

Directionless, Passive Men

THIS SEEMS TO be a new trend. A nearby university now has about two-thirds women and one-third men. More guys are graduating from high school with no clue of what they want to be when they grow up. They coasted through school and now they are still living at home while they try to find themselves. Living at home is not a problem for awhile. I know a few guys in that position right now and they are not losers. A grown man still living at home is, however, a yellow warning flag that should make you take a closer look at that man's ambition, dreams, and future.

I have a friend at a university who has worked in counseling college students for 20 years. He reports this observation of a trend in college men. For many guys, their life consists of video games, porn, and maybe working out. That's about it. It's all self-focused pleasure. They must study sometime, but just because a guy is in college does not mean he has ambition or purpose in life.

What Do Passive Guys Do? Whatever.

Passive guys have top dating ideas like these: Watch a movie and hang out, rent a movie and hang out, eat and hang out, play video games and hang out. Some hanging out is fine; all hanging out is a problem.

The reason passivity might matter to you is that many men, including the good ones, have a tendency to become passive in the family. Men can pour so much of themselves into their work that they just want to shut down when they get home. The wife is empathetic and capable, so she picks up the slack. The more she does, the less he does. Eventually, the family schedule, kid's homework, putting kids to bed, child discipline, the anniversary date, and most of the family life decisions fall on her shoulders. On the one hand, this might seem good because you, the wife, get to do what you want and call the shots. On the other hand, you may end up feeling overburdened because you are making many of the tough decisions of life by yourself and doing most of the work. Passive daters become passive husbands and passive fathers. Don't expect miraculous behavior changes. What you see is probably what you will get.

Savvy wives and girlfriends learn how to encourage the guy to take the initiative and assume responsibility for certain aspects of how you spend your time together. Much of this involves giving positive feedback for his good decisions and showing him respect as much as possible. Men thrive on respect; a language they understand. If you are with a prince, he should be generally respectable. Every woman in every relationship needs to hone skills of positive encouragement. You will benefit by them now and later in marriage. Guys don't respond well to nagging, the most common method used by women in their attempt to alter men's behavior. Practice with methods that work early in the relationship.

Chapter 75

Dating for the Worst Time in Your Life

A FEW YEARS ago Ruth and I took a brief trip to Europe to see part of Germany and France. The grand finale was a day and night in Paris that we had both dreamed of. I picked out a cute area near the Eiffel Tower and started looking for a place to stay. After dragging our luggage to 5 or 6 no vacancy hotels, I was becoming concerned. Eventually, Ruth plopped down at a sidewalk café as I jogged up and down the streets using my pathetic French, "Avez vous la room?" All the time the minutes were ticking away from our brief visit in Paris.

Finally, sweating and defeated, I came back without a room for us. We sat down to figure out what we could do. We decided to take the metro to a less popular area and found a tiny room, but most of the day was lost. I was upset with myself and disappointed at the loss of our only day in Paris. Ruth could see my low spirits. She smiled and told me how much she had enjoyed the coffee at the café and how wonderful the trip had been. She said she was happy no matter what happened in Paris. I instantly felt relieved. Maybe I wasn't a loser after all. I was ready to live out a long time dream, to kiss my wife on a bridge in Paris. Prior to her encouragement, I was about to spoil the little time we had left in Paris, but then I realized we had the entire evening to enjoy ourselves and that magnificent setting. At that low moment I was so thankful that I had married someone who could pick me up and reassure me that she thought I was wonderful, no matter what.

Unconditional love and acceptance are critical traits that you can look for in your potential spouse. If an important trait is absent while you are dating, don't expect it to appear after you are married. Life will pull you down plenty so be sure you choose a boyfriend who will pick you up, not drag you down.

Most of life is not a carefully-planned date. Life is ordinary activities that do not go as planned. Work and family obligations are often inconvenient, and countless situations arise in which we are required to do what we really don't want to do. Relationships are filled with compromises. If you need to carefully orchestrate activities and situations to make sure that everything goes just right for your boyfriend, you are in for a lifetime of trials.

> *If an important trait is absent while you are dating, don't expect it to appear after you are married.*

That is why typical dates such as dinner and a movie, watching videos, and just hanging out do not help you evaluate the guy very well. Eating, watching videos, and hanging out are not important life skills most of the time. Review the "Creative Dating" chapter for creative date ideas.

Chapter 76

Online Toad Sorting

eharmony.com, match.com, etc.

Pros and Cons of Online Matchmaking

Pros

ONLINE MATCHMAKING IS an efficient way to sift through a lot of people and not waste time on guys who are clearly not compatible. You can start out with someone with whom you know you have a few things in common. You might spend time writing to each other and getting to know each other as friends before you ever meet. Meg Ryan and Tom Hanks did this in the movie *You've Got Mail* and it seemed to work for them.

Cons

Often online matches are long-distance relationships, so there is a lot of pressure when you finally meet. There would also be a tendency to compress the courtship or rush things because you may only have limited time together.

I would not trust anyone met in a chat room because the anonymity allows people to say or become anything they want. The slimiest guy can guess what you would like to hear and write beautiful, sensitive messages that have nothing to do with his true character. He could be a fat, bald,

40-year-old man living in his parents' basement but he claims to be a 25-year-old paramedic who loves to surf while he works on his masters degree and volunteers at the orphanage.

No Intuition

Many women have a well-developed intuition that can help them detect unsavory people. It occurs subconsciously as they watch body language, facial expressions, eye movement, voice intonation, and general mannerisms. Although not completely reliable, intuition is helpful in most situations; however, intuition is not possible through the computer keyboard.

Summary

Online dating can be a reasonable tool to help meet guys. As the ratio of princes to toads gets worse, the use of this technology might become more and more important to help you meet like-minded people. You may be able to detect some toads with the keyboard, but most people disclose their best traits online and leave the warts for you to discover in person. If you can filter your online search based on critical factors such as attitudes about sex or spiritual beliefs, you can at least narrow your field to guys who are more likely to be compatible with you. Sex and God are such defining elements of a person's character that a person's attitude toward either subject provides powerful tools to evaluate critical factors. Just remember that once you meet him, the rest of the relational concepts and pitfalls in this book are the same.

Chapter 77

To Find the Right Person, Be the Right Person

PEOPLE ARE USUALLY attracted to people who are similar to them in social status and character quality. Men of high character look for women of high character. Christian men look for Christian women. Muslim men look for Muslim women. Intelligent men want intelligent women with whom they can communicate readily. Compassionate, caring men admire women with those traits. Be sure to cultivate your personal growth in the important areas, so that you will be appealing to the quality guys.

If you do not have a special hobby or interest, find one. If you need help, brainstorm a list, read some books, join a club, and follow something that interests you. Become an expert at something. Only you can know what that is. Take dance lessons. Consider volunteering somewhere. A special hobby or interest will make you more interesting and you will find other people (men) with similar interests or similar compassions. The mere fact that you are there will give you a head start at being the right person.

If You Want a Man of Integrity, You Must Be a Woman of Integrity

What do I mean by integrity? A person of integrity is someone who not only talks about doing the right thing, but strives to do the right thing. This person has a moral or ethical foundation that guides him or her in daily decisions. Although obviously not perfect, a person of integrity is who he/she is when no one's looking. This person would be a spouse you can rely on through the difficulties of life and marriage.

Chapter 78

The Big Three

Love, Sex, and Money

IF YOU LEARN to navigate these three major elements of human-ity—love, sex, and money—you will do well in life. These are the major stumbling blocks for people in any culture or situation. Virtually everyone, male and female, wants all three. How we get them and what we do if we don't get them makes the difference between satisfaction and dissatisfaction with life.

Sex and love tend to get confused and intertwined to the point that people think they are interchangeable. Men and women have some differences in dealing with the two. Women are more likely to make mistakes because of their strong desire to find the love of a man. Men are more likely to make their mistakes because of their desire for the physical pleasure of sex. The sexes are probably about equal in their money struggles. Too much money or not enough money can be a problem, but money advice is for another book.

Women Give Sex to Get Love; Men Give Love to Get Sex

Obviously women enjoy sex, and men want to be loved; however, when it comes to doing something foolish, each gender has its own weakness. Women mistakenly believe that the guy loves her because they have sex or that having sex will make him love her. Sorry, sex is not necessarily related to love in the simple mind of a man.

Men mistakenly believe that they are in love with the woman when they are really in love with the pleasure she provides. Men then mistakenly marry their bundle of pleasure and are surprised later in the marriage that they didn't actually love her as a person apart from her body. She too, might be surprised by the same revelation because in her female mind, the sex proved their love for each other.

These classic errors continue to cause pain, regret, and divorce for the naive. If you do not come to an accurate understanding of the connection between love and sex, I predict great pain in your future. However, there is also great freedom and reward when you know the truth. The truth is that love trumps everything. You can have little money, no sex, and no husband and still know genuine love that leads to a totally satisfying life. That is the good news.

To explore this concept in greater depth, visit FindingYourPrince. com.

Chapter 79

"So sad to belong to someone else when the right one comes along."

ENGLAND DAN & JOHN FORD COLEY (70S POP MUSIC)

MANY WOMEN LOOK at another woman with a boyfriend and wish they had someone to be with. They assume that these women must be okay because someone has chosen them as a companion. Often these thoughts extend to the belief that you must be a loser because you do not have a boyfriend. In fact, you might have no prospects at all. There is no correlation between boyfriend status and loser status.

Some women try to soothe their insecurity by entering an exclusive relationship at the first opportunity. This makes her feel wanted for the moment. Instead of sitting at home alone or hanging out with the girls, she is comforted to know she will have a date for Saturday night. However, if the companion is not really long-term material, she is taking herself out of the pool of available single women. A truly wonderful guy could come along and will write her off even though there was some initial attraction because she is already attached. That opportunity could be lost forever.

Getting exclusive is usually a mistake unless you are becoming convinced that you are with a guy who could be your future spouse. Having a boyfriend for comfort and esteem is a short-term fix, but it is a poor strategy for the long haul. A lot of decent guys might cross your path while you are wasting your time with a relationship that is going nowhere. Your time is too valuable to squander this way.

Chapter 80

You Will Marry Gutterslime. I Did

WE MARRY PEOPLE like ourselves. I married gutterslime because I am gutterslime. On the outside, I may look like a respectable veterinarian. On the inside, I am the only one who knows all the things I have done when no one was looking, all the compromises and shortcuts that no one would ever know, all my backstabbing comments, all of my lies, all the women I have looked at and contemplated. The list could go on. That is just this morning. I am pathetic.

I do not usually introduce Ruth as my gutterslime wife, but I could. When I first started seeing Ruth, I thought she was almost perfect. The more time we spent together, the more flaws I saw. I could make you a list. The longer we are married, the more I know of her flaws. We have chosen to love each other in spite of our flaws. Regardless of the glossy image we try to project for the world, if we truly analyze ourselves and our motives, it is an ugly picture. That, unfortunately, is the way people are—princes, toads, everyone. Your prince will have warts and even a toad will have some admirable qualities. Remember, your man should be predominantly prince, and you must strive to recognize most of his warts and gutterslime flaws before you get married, so you can decide if you are willing to live with these flaws.

I have enough confidence to write a book full of advice about relationships, but much of my advice comes from the dark side of me that I do not broadcast to the general public. I can report with authority on the way males think because I have been one all of my life. Most of the thoughts and traits of men I discuss with insight because I have either done them or considered doing them. Women are just as bad as men but in their own feminine way.

What happens when two balls of gutterslime get married? They have problems. Marriage is difficult because both people are guaranteed to have significant flaws. The flaws create friction and arguments. Even the two nicest, best-matched people in the world will have some very rough times. It comes with the territory of living together and sharing all the bumps of life intimately.

There are a thousand influences working to pull even the best marriage apart. Some of the stresses are fatigue, disappointment, workaholism, football, hunting, children conflicts, lost jobs, forced moves, pornography, affairs (mental or physical), money struggles (too much or not enough), unrealistic sex expectations, family/in-law stress, arguments, alcohol, physical abuse, silence, anger, etc. This is a scary list. Read it through again because this is part of your motivation to consider carefully whether or not my radical advice, especially about sex, is valid. My analogies and word pictures are only wacky to help you remember them. The message itself is as serious as a heart attack.

It is to your benefit to do all that you can to give yourself the best chances for success in your marriage. You will need all the help you can get. Two of the most important factors to get right are 1) choosing the right person to start with and 2) not collecting emotional baggage in your singleness that you will lug through your entire marriage. Many people are well aware of the sexually transmitted diseases that can be dragged into a marriage and cause hardship, but the emotional baggage can be even more damaging.

> When asked his secret of love, being married fifty-four years to the same person, he said, "Ruth and I are happily incompatible."
>
> —Billy Graham

... and when asked if she ever considered divorce from Billy,
Ruth replied, "Divorce no, murder yes."

—Ruth Graham

Chapter 81

Is That a Wart on Your Nose?

Perhaps You Are a Female Toad

SINCE THIS BOOK is directed to women, I have given you the benefit of the doubt and assumed that you are a princess. To be fair to men, I must acknowledge that women can be just as toxic and toadlike as men. Some women are master manipulators who can reel in a guy and proceed to make his life miserable. The list of troublesome traits in women is just as long as the list for men. I hope you do not have too many of those female toad traits.

A female toad is a high-maintenance woman to whom no man would want to be married for a lifetime. She insists that life happens her way. If she is unhappy, those around her must know about it and share in her misery. Manipulation is one of the most common toad traits that I observe in women. They can manipulate with mind games, clever words, or attitudes to get their way. Many girls discover the sexual power they possess and use it to control or influence men. Clothing, cleavage, innuendo, sensual touch, or blatant sex can have tremendous influence on men, often enticing men to their destruction, like moths to a flame.

She may be a beautiful toad and her beauty magically causes people to cater to her whims. Unwise or unlucky men may fall under her spell. Men may be blinded to her character warts because of her outer beauty, her generous sex attitude, or her manipulation skills. Once the thrill wears off, it's misery for everyone. Note: Female toads may not recognize themselves in the above description.

Another way that women can grow toad warts is by hanging out with toads. A woman who is sexually active with a toad is not only giving away pieces of her heart, she is also gaining emotional warts with each encounter. This reduces her appeal to a prince. If you spend your time with the toads, a prince might mistake you for a female toad.

"Show me your friends and I'll show you your future."

—Randy Droughon

Chapter 82

Lifestyles of the Rich and Famous and Confused

CELEBRITIES ARE UNRELIABLE role models for relationships. The combination of wealth, celebrity, and sex drive creates such a confusing maze of questionable motives that I would hate to be in the shoes of beautiful, single celebrities. They face an overwhelming task to untangle the complex web of motives for anyone relationally interested in them. Celebrities have the same dream as you have—to find love that will last a lifetime, yet they may easily be even more confused than you. The number of celebrities at the rehab center, divorce court, scientology building, and psychologist's clinic suggests celebs probably need an extra chapter for their unique and perilous situation. I am certainly not the guru for celebrities but I know they are just as human as you and me and will hurt just as much as a regular person when their relationship implodes. Don't be fooled by the smile and the BMW. Examine their advice and example cautiously.

Good Advice from Celebrities

"Marriage is the hardest thing you will ever do. The secret is removing divorce as an option. Anybody who gives themselves that option will get a divorce."

—Will Smith *(11 years into his second marriage)*

As for his secret to staying married: "My wife tells me that if I ever decide to leave, she is coming with me."

—Jon BonJovi

The happiest times in my life were when my relationships were going well—when I was in love with someone, and someone was loving me. But in my whole life, I haven't met the person I can sustain a relationship with yet. So I'm discontented about that. I'm angry with myself. I have regrets. You don't get hugged by the Rock and Roll Hall of Fame, and you don't have children with the Rock and Roll Hall of Fame. I want what everybody else wants: to love and to be loved, and to have a family.

—Billy Joel, *The New York Times Magazine 9/02*

Chapter 83

The Key to a Man's Heart (Not What You Think)

ONE OF THE foundational needs of a man is to know that he is respected. Men need to know that they are significant, that their opinion matters, that they are adequate and up to the task, and that they are competent. These needs are consistent through their occupation, school, marriage, relationships, and sports. A woman who understands these needs has a great advantage. Many women automatically assume that since they have a deep need to feel loved, cherished, and cared for, men feel the same way. Although men need these to some degree, in reality, showing a man respect is one of the most effective ways of demonstrating love to him.

Understanding these different needs (to be loved for a woman and to be respected for a man) is critical for husbands and wives if they plan to really know about each other. We discuss it in our premarital counseling. Single women need to understand this too. If a man knows he is respected by you, he will find you more attractive. Your subtle eye roll or cutting remark, even if you are just kidding, will reduce your standing with him. Respect is a language that men understand.

The different needs of men and women is a large topic. A great book on the subject is *Love and Respect* by Emerson Eggerich. *Love and Respect* will help you in any part of your life where you interact with men, but it is especially helpful for married couples when they are trying to figure out why they are driving each other crazy. Men think radically differently from you. If you understand this, you are empowered.

Chapter 84

Every Divorce Starts with a Kiss

You May Kiss the Bride

EVERY WEDDING ALBUM is the same. Each one is filled with photos of a happy couple smiling, kissing, feeding each other cake, gazing with soft focus at a ring, blah blah blah. Each couple is filled with elation that they know they have this wonderful, beautiful, loving partner with whom they will spend the rest of their life. Honeymoon passion is next, then a lifetime of bliss together. Virtually every marriage begins this way. Yet, 5 out of 10 will end up in divorce with bitterness, hate, and deep emotional wounds. What happened? People don't enter a marriage expecting a divorce. Most people believe that they are immune. Their relationship will be different.

No one could look at a wedding album and predict the future happiness of the couple. I am always fascinated to see Hollywood couples getting married. That beautiful couple couldn't have been happier. We read all about their secrets of love in a *Cosmopolitan* article. How many are divorced now? They keep giving advice while their world is falling apart, yet we see their little snapshot of marital bliss and want to hear all of their wisdom for healthy relationships. These articles are the primary source of relational wisdom for a lot of people.

And so it goes with many of our sources of information. Girls who happen to have a boyfriend think they know guys. They are a momentary

251

authority because they look like they have successfully landed a man. Flirtatious girls who talk to boys easily and seem to be popular could tell you all their important secrets about boys. Even a cheerful family at Disney World® can look absolutely happy on the outside and the marriage is falling apart behind closed doors. I know this sounds depressing. The point is that there are many unreliable sources of information and wisdom for relationships.

I would argue that most of our modern culture is quite confused about relationships; however, most people are boldly and confidently messing up their lives as they plunge in with all the wisdom they have gleaned from *People* and *Cosmo.* Yet, thousands of girls want to dress, dance, and emulate the celebrity of the week who is likely headed to rehab next week. Argh!

In Defense of Britany

At the time of this writing, Britany Spear's life is in free fall as she self-destructs before the paparazzi cameras. How did she get to this point? In Britany's defense, she is a colorful example of how girls are commonly exploited. Britany started out as this wonderfully talented, beautiful Mouseketeer who broke into the pop music market. Life was good. Somewhere, someone convinced her to start taking off most of her clothes and dancing very sensually. She was good at it. Boys were mesmerized. Girls wanted to emulate her. She was following someone's advice to crank up her sexual image. She became very popular and landed herself a worthless, low-life husband. Who knows where she will be by the time you read this book.

Any girl in the world can follow the advice of pop culture, and I guarantee that you will find yourself a man. Sex is the one absolute way to get a man, but what kind of man will you end up with? If you are willing to offer sexual favors, there will be males interested in you. Colleges are loaded with women who will have sex or agree to sexual activity. Some stats say that 60% of college women are sexually active. Since so many are having casual sex outside of marriage, it seems normal. If done tastefully, it even seems dignified. Is this the path to finding a husband?

Plenty of toads in America are willing to have sex with you if you are willing. You may think that you are being discerning, but you only fool yourself. Many women are giving themselves away for the price of some smooth words, some personal attention, and a guy who is interested long enough to sleep with them. Every relationship begins with optimism, good intentions, and probably a kiss. It can take years to see how things are really going. True love is a marathon, not a sprint.

Chapter 85

Spiritual Compatibility

FOR PEOPLE WHO hold specific spiritual beliefs, spiritual compatibility becomes just as important as emotional, personal, and physical compatibility. If you are committed to a particular faith, it makes no sense to dismiss that faith for a guy. Either the faith is true and more important than any man, or it is false and not worth your time in the first place. Some faiths such as Christianity are so central to a person's life that his/her entire belief system, worldview, and character traits flow from it. If you are a Christian and marry someone who does not share your faith, you will either abandon your faith or attend church with your children and without your husband. An important part of your life would split the family, and this is certainly not the best situation for a family.

If you honestly believe the Bible to be true, it would be tragic to walk away from your faith and it would be tragic to split the family. If your faith defines who you are, you should be dating guys with similar beliefs. If you compromise and date a really nice guy who is not spiritually compatible with you, you will be in a bind if it turns out that you really like each other.

In the same way, a practicing Muslim would probably want to marry a practicing Muslim to create unity in the home. Again, family life becomes more difficult when children are part of the picture if the dad undermines the credibility of the religion by his lack of participation.

If you have no strong spiritual beliefs, this may not be an issue for you. Without a spiritual belief system, you and your partner will do whatever seems best in your own eyes, composing your own individual versions of truth, and right vs. wrong. When both partners use the same spiritual reference, unity is more likely to be found.

Something's Got to Give

You might argue, "We're not getting married, we're just going to a movie," but if he turns out to be a really special guy, you will certainly want to get a little closer. Eventually you will be at the fork in the road between the guy and the beliefs you have professed as the foundation of your life. Your problem will be solved if he converts to your religion; however, dating conversions are rare and unpredictable. If he converts only for your sake, without true belief, you have created a shallow hypocrite. The guy will find it very difficult to analyze his true motivations and beliefs. Would he follow the religion even if you broke up? I know of a few solid marriages in which a spouse genuinely adopted a new faith during the courtship. It can happen, but an important compatibility factor is left in doubt.

You Mate How You Date

If you date men who are outside your faith, you will likely marry a man who is outside your faith. We mate how we date. Your decision in this area is probably a good indicator of the sincerity of your own beliefs.

Chapter 86

An Impossible Journey?

Frodo's Epic Journey

A FEW YEARS ago J.R.R. Tolkien's classic book, *Lord of the Rings*, was made into a movie. In this story, the main character, Frodo, is an ordinary guy who is given a gold ring with mysterious powers and he embarks on a perilous journey to deliver the ring into a fiery volcano to save the world.

Your journey to obtain a wedding ring with a happy, lifelong marriage is filled with as much excitement (falling in love) and peril (getting dumped or burned) as Frodo's mission to deliver and destroy his ring. Your missions are similar:

- Frodo understood he had an important mission that could change his life forever.
  - Love and sex decisions are life altering.
- Frodo understood the risks but considered the goal to be worth the risks.
  - A great marriage is a noble and worthy goal.
- Frodo knew he must take a path that is different from many others.
  - Most people are clueless and irrational in pursuit of love.

- When obstacles seemed insurmountable, Frodo pressed on without compromising the mission.
  - Compromising your standards when you are lonely or desperate will jeopardize your true mission of marriage.
- Frodo was well aware of higher forces of good and evil at work around him and within him. Gollum/Smeagol, the hunched crawling guy who ate the live fish, would transform instantly from a helpful guide to a hideous creature. Sauron, the top evil guy, had a broad plan to gain power and had no interest in anything good. Orcs, toads, followed Sauron blindly and were very dangerous. Gandalf was a force of good. At the most critical moments, Gandalf provided supernatural support that enabled Frodo to survive the confrontation, so that he could ultimately succeed in his mission.
  - You will feel pressure from other women, men, and your own internal yearnings to abandon your convictions.

Your goal may be to find your prince and live happily ever after. Your life, however, is not a movie so there is no guarantee it will turn out the way you hope. Fortunately, your real success and happiness in life does not depend on finding your prince; it depends on how you live each day of the journey.

Fortunately, your real success and happiness in life does not depend on finding your prince; it depends on how you live each day of the journey.

Your Epic Journey—Tough But Not Impossible

One—find a worthy prince among a vast sea of toads.

Two—Build a loving intimate relationship with him, sharing your innermost thoughts, feelings, dreams, weaknesses, and fears.

Three—Even though your emotional, relational, and spiritual intimacy draw you closer to one another, you must resist the overwhelming urge to become sexually intimate until married.

Four—Make a lifetime decision about marriage based on unpredictable changes that may occur in yourself and your man.

Yikes! That is more intimidating than the thousands of Orcs in the final battle scene of *Lord of the Rings*..

You Might Need More Than a Plan

A recipe for success is important but it might leave you a little short. Would Frodo have succeeded without the help of Gandalf? Only Tolkien knows for sure. Frodo needed help and you probably do too. Many people find inner strength, security, and a sense of purpose through their faith.

Faith can strengthen convictions and give a person the power to show restraint when they are tempted to do activities that would be exhilarating at the moment but regrettable in the future. People who believe in God can pray for wisdom or strength to enable them to withstand temptation.

A Twelve-Step Program

Before someone enters a program to overcome substance abuse or addictive behavior, they must first admit that they have a problem and need help to overcome whatever holds them down. You probably do not need a twelve-step program, but for some women, the intense desire for a relationship with a guy can rule over them and pull them down. They have a problem. We can all learn a few things about overcoming obstacles from successful rehab programs.

Another requirement of most twelve-step programs is that participants must acknowledge the existence of a higher power—something bigger than they. Spiritual power is mentioned in several of the twelve steps.

Throughout this book, we have talked about human nature, emotions, and physical desires but there is another critical human dimension needed to complete the puzzle—our spiritual nature. People are naturally spiritual beings. Most people in any civilization or culture have a sense that there is a higher power. They might not be confident about the power but an inner voice tells them there is something bigger than them be it God, Allah, or Buddha, as well as Scientology, animal worship, Hawaiian gods, New Age mysticism, ancient human sacrifice, or Greek gods. The list is long.

Atheists would be the exception because, by definition, they do not believe any higher power exists; however, even an atheist has a belief system. His world might revolve around himself or some belief system he believes to be logical. It actually requires a tremendous level of faith to confidently reject all sense of God, so whether he admits it or not, every person is religious.

Ask anyone what they believe and they will tell you. Everyone believes something; however, all belief systems are not created equal. If you believe in the power of a rock, that might be helpful to some degree for positive thinking, but the rock itself is not really doing anything for you. I happen to believe that God is real, true, living, and a powerful force in people's lives.

Just as Frodo benefited from Gandalf's power and alcoholics gain strength from God to battle their addiction, you may find that a spiritual foundation is helpful or even essential to enable you to face the challenges of dating relationships. Your own willpower may not be enough.

Read more about the spiritual foundation of relationships at FindingYourPrince.com

All the Best

I HOPE YOU are optimistic after reading this book. Knowledge is power and you are empowered by a better understanding of the many unspoken dynamics in male/female relationships. Regardless of any previous botched relationships or disappointment with your love life, I hope you feel encouraged not only about your future, but particularly about the hope that you will one day find a great husband—your prince. You can actually enjoy the adventure ahead without fear because you know the most common pitfalls to avoid. As you improve and use your conversation skills, your confidence will grow along with the friendships you build with men or other women. Enjoy each day of the journey now and don't panic about your future. Your future is bright. I wish you all the best with your life's journey.

FindingYourPrince.com

Ten Important
Research Findings on
Marriage and Choosing
a Marriage Partner

Helpful Facts for Young Adults
From the National Marriage Project

1. **Marrying as a teenager is the highest known risk factor for divorce.**

   People who marry in their teens are two to three times more likely to divorce than people who marry in their twenties or older.

2. **The most likely way to find a future marriage partner is through an introduction by family, friends, or acquaintances.**

   Despite the romantic notion that people meet and fall in love through chance or fate, the evidence suggests that social networks are important in bringing together individuals of similar interests and backgrounds, especially when it comes to selecting a marriage partner. According to a large-scale national survey of sexuality, almost sixty percent of married people were introduced by family, friends, coworkers, or other acquaintances.

3. **The more similar people are in their values, backgrounds, and life goals, the more likely they will have a successful marriage.**

Opposites may attract but they may not live together harmoniously as married couples. People who share common backgrounds and similar social networks are better suited as marriage partners than people who are very different in their backgrounds and networks.

4. **Women have a significantly better chance of marrying if they do not become single parents before marrying.**

Having a child out of wedlock reduces the chances of ever marrying. Despite the growing numbers of potential marriage partners with children, one study noted, "having children is still one of the least desirable characteristics a potential marriage partner can possess." The only partner characteristic men and women rank as even less desirable than having children is the inability to hold a steady job.

5. **Both women and men who are college educated are more likely to marry, and less likely to divorce, than people with lower levels of education.**

Despite occasional news stories predicting lifelong singlehood for college-educated women, these predictions have proven false. Though the first generation of college-educated women (those who earned baccalaureate degrees in the 1920s) married less frequently than their less well-educated peers, the reverse is true today. College-educated women's chances of marrying are better than less well-educated women. However, the growing gender gap in college education may make it more difficult for college women to find similarly well-educated men in the future. This is already a problem for African-American female college graduates, who greatly outnumber African-American male college graduates.

6. Living together before marriage has not proven useful as a "trial marriage."

People who have multiple cohabiting relationships before marriage are more likely to experience marital conflict, marital unhappiness, and eventual divorce than people who do not cohabit before marriage. Researchers attribute some but not all of these differences to the differing characteristics of people who cohabit, the so-called "selection effect," rather than to the experience of cohabiting itself. It has been hypothesized that the negative effects of cohabitation on future marital success may diminish as living together becomes a common experience among today's young adults. However, according to one recent study of couples who were married between 1981 and 1997, the negative effects persist among younger cohorts, supporting the view that the cohabitation experience itself contributes to problems in marriage.

7. Marriage helps people generate income and wealth.

Compared to those who merely live together, people who marry become economically better off. Men become more productive after marriage; they earn between ten and forty percent more than do single men with similar education and job histories. Marital social norms that encourage healthy, productive behavior and wealth accumulation play a role. Some of the greater wealth of married couples results from their more efficient specialization and pooling of resources, and because they save more. Married people also receive more money from family members than the unmarried (including cohabiting couples), probably because families consider marriage more permanent and more binding than a living-together union.

8. People who are married are more likely to have emotionally and physically satisfying sex lives than single people or those who live together.

Contrary to the popular belief that married sex is boring and infrequent, married people report higher levels of sexual satisfaction than both sexually active singles and cohabiting couples, according to the most comprehensive and recent survey of sexuality. Forty-two percent of wives said that they found sex extremely emotionally and physically satisfying, compared to just 31 percent of single women who had a sex partner. And 48 percent of husbands said sex was extremely satisfying emotionally, compared to just 37 percent of cohabiting men. The higher level of commitment in marriage is probably the reason for the high level of reported sexual satisfaction. Marital commitment contributes to a greater sense of trust and security, less drug and alcohol-infused sex, and more mutual communication between the couple.

9. People who grow up in a family broken by divorce are slightly less likely to marry, and much more likely to divorce when they do marry.

According to one study the divorce risk nearly triples if one marries someone who also comes from a broken home. The increased risk is much lower, however, if the marital partner is someone who grew up in a happy, intact family.

10. For large segments of the population, the risk of divorce is far below fifty percent.

Although the overall divorce rate in America remains close to fifty percent of all marriages, it has been dropping gradually over the past two decades. Also, the risk of divorce is far below fifty percent for educated people going into their first marriage, and lower still for people who wait to marry at least until their mid-twenties, haven't lived with many different partners prior to marriage, or are strongly religious and marry someone of the same faith.

Chapter Summaries

TO HELP YOU REMEMBER THE KEY POINTS OF EACH CHAPTER

Damsel in Distress—Why you need this book

1. Finding Your Prince in a Sea of Toads—There are still good men out there. You should spend most of your time with princes rather than with toads. Without a rational plan, conventional practices will lead you to many toads and cause much unnecessary pain.
2. Princes and Toads—All guys are a combination of prince and toad. You want mostly "prince" and must decide what warts you can live with.
3. Once a Toad, Always a Toad?—Anyone can experience a radical change in their life and transform from a jerk to a wonderful person. The change must happen without your help. Don't try to fix a toad.
4. True Confessions—The Author is a Fake. Actually the author just has unexpected credentials. Question my authority. Question all authorities. You must determine what is true because many conventional authorities could be wrong. Only you live with the consequences of bad advice.
5. A Skull Full of Mush—Think it through before you are in a relationship because you may not think clearly once you are in one.

267

6. Roadkill!—Just because some marriages succeed, doesn't mean their methods were wise. Don't play Russian roulette with your relationships. You are responsible for your own life choices.
7. The Plan—So Simple, So Powerful
   a. Learn to talk with guys—Your power lies here. No matter how pathetic you are now, conversation is a learned skill and you can be an expert if you choose. Communicating well with guys is an essential skill for dating and marriage.
   b. Don't sleep with him. This is the most common and most damaging dating mistake you can make for lots of reasons you have never heard before. However, avoiding sleeping with him is much harder to do than you expect.
   c. Don't panic. Many women toss rational thinking to the wind because they fear they will be single forever.

Learn to Talk with Guys

8. Communication—Your Most Important Skill. Invest the effort to improve your communication skills and you will boost your confidence and enjoyment in dating.
9. LIPS, Your Secret Weapon—Learning to converse with guys is one of your most important skills.
10. Practice on Someone You Don't Care About—Practice conversation with people who are safe and with whom you have no romantic interest so you are ready when someone interesting comes along.
11. Smile—Get comfortable with your smile and learn to use it anytime you choose. Smiles enhance your attractiveness.
12. High School Strategy—Don't bother with an exclusive relationship in high school. Enjoy being around guys and learn to be comfortable with them, but they are not ready for a real relationship ... yet.
13. Fateful Attraction—Attraction cannot be forced or faked but it *can* be influenced. There are three kinds of attraction—one kind can grow, two kinds will fade.

14. The Beauty Curse—Hopefully you're not too pretty. Most women strive for beauty but it can cause some difficulties.

15. Dogs Chase Cars—Pursuing guys sends lots of wrong messages.

16. Flirting—Subtle flirting may be okay. Replace flirting with interesting conversation.

17. Chance Meetings—Subtle actions that can increase your chance of contact.

18. First Date—Here's some insight into how a guy thinks.

19. Non-Dating—Well-chosen time together can eliminate much of the stress and pain of dating. It can be enjoyable, rewarding, and safe.

20. Creative Dating—Find out more about a guy in a single activity than a dozen movie dates and have less stress.

21. How to Dump a Guy Humanely—Men like to be told the truth, so hit him right between the eyes with it if you are no longer interested.

22. Never Say I Love You—These words have serious meaning but most people are clueless.

Don't Sleep with Him

WHY NOT

23. Baffled by Instinct—Humans are rational creatures in almost all areas, but we become very confused by our mysterious sexual urges.

24. Recipe For Success—Some relationship mistakes can have predictably negative results.

25. Who Are You?—Are you okay with casual sex, okay with sex in a committed relationship, or okay with sex only in marriage?

26. You Can't Put a Condom on Your Heart—Your heart is at risk and a condom won't protect you from emotionally risky sex.

27. Sex Is Like Duct Tape—Sex is meant to help one couple bond together permanently for life. Each time it is used outside of marriage, it loses some of its stickiness.

28. Intended for Pleasure—Sex is part of the superglue for marriage. Surfaces must be clean and dry for good adherence.

29. A Pretend Marriage—Living together does not improve your chances for a satisfying marriage and has serious risks.

30. Try Before You Buy—Having sex to confirm that you are compatible will not work.

31. Men Are Microwaves, Women Are Crockpots—Men respond very quickly sexually and women respond more slowly. It is important to understand this before and after you are married. Learn why.

32. Ghosts in My Bed—Sexual memories get stashed in a special section of the brain that is slow to forget. Memories of previous sex partners will follow you right into bed with your husband whether you want them there or not. His past partners will be there too.

33. Friends with Benefits—If you treat your sexuality like a meaningless toy, that's what it will become.

34. Sags, Bulges, and Wrinkles—Your body is on its way downhill so how do you know if he will still love you when you plump up like a Ballpark Frank.

35. Boyfriend Bait—Guaranteed to Work—Any female is guaranteed to attract a male if she is willing to have sex with him.

36. All Men Are Sex Maniacs—Men's sex drive is a good thing but you must understand it or get burned.

37. Women Want Sex As Much As Men—This is not quite true. Women have urges that are just as powerful as men's, but women yearn for true, complete relationships. Men yearn for the physical pleasure of sex.

38. A Million Dollar Bowl of Cheerios®—Know the huge difference between the true value of your sexuality and the way it is commonly viewed by men.

39. Women Have Been Duped—Women have been tricked into giving up sex. It took awhile, but men have pulled a fast one on you.

40. Physics of Sex—Sex can be the greatest pleasure known to humans but it also has the potential for the greatest pain.

41. You Would Do Just Fine—Many guys are simply looking for a place to deposit their sperm and they do not care who the recipient might be.

42. The Girls All Get Prettier at Closing Time—Some men will make a lot of shallow compromises to have sex.

43. "You Can't Handle the Truth"—You can't handle the pleasure. Sex is more powerful than people expect so it has many unexpected consequences. People over-estimate their self-control and self-awareness.

44. Why Girls Don't Play in the NFL—Women are made differently than men. A woman would get creamed playing football and she can be hurt sexually in situations that have little impact on the man.

45. Men Are Waffles, Women Are Spaghetti—This edible analogy is why the football statement is true. Men can compartmentalize their sexuality so it does not necessarily affect the other parts of their life or self-esteem. A woman's sexuality is so complex, it is automatically entangled with every other part of her being and self-esteem.

46. Numbed—Overwhelming emotional pain can cause you to shut down your emotions in order to relieve the pain.

47. I Can't Get No Satisfaction—Staying satisfied with your spouse is the key to prevent divorce. Sex while single may reduce long-term satisfaction.

48. Single Sex vs. Married Sex—The act is the same but the results are entirely different for unmarried couples compared to married couples.

49. What's Love Got to Do With It?—Love has everything to do with it. Love is king when it is true love.

50. It's Just a Bunny—From *Monty Python's Holy Grail*, sex while single looks soft, cuddly, desirable, and harmless but it actually has huge fangs.

51. Porn—Pornography is ruining lots of men at this very moment. It is a huge marriage killer. You must understand how this affects men and how it can ruin your marriage. You have no idea.

52. The Love Test—Herein lies a simple, reliable test to help evaluate if he really loves you. This test is an excellent toad detector.
53. More Clues about Your Man from the Love Test—How much does he love you? The answer is revealed by how much he would sacrifice to win you or protect you. Will he put your needs above his desires?
54. STDs—Do the Math. The statistics are not in your favor. Roll the dice. Play for life.

Don't Sleep with Him

HOW NOT

55. Now the Hard Part—Not having sex before marriage is a lot harder than you may think.
56. Hug the Wall—We only take precautions when we perceive a risk. If you do not recognize the risks, you can easily slide into sex when you never intended to.
57. Simply Irresistible—This section discusses things that are off limits and things that are new or enticing.
58. The One-Way Road of Passion—Explore how we move from eye contact to intercourse—the one-way stepwise progression of physical intimacy. Where is the point of no return?
59. It's Just a Matter of Time—As a dating couple accumulates time together, they will naturally get closer and closer to having sex unless they take steps to prevent it.
60. The Red Zone—Certain activities and circumstances will make physical intimacy more likely.
61. Who Plugged In My Crockpot?—Women can be surprised by their own intense sexual yearning when they are deeply attracted to a guy.
62. Does Somebody Need a Hug?—You do, just as all girls do. If you don't get it from your dad, you need it from somewhere. Don't hug a toad.
63. Civilized Women: Good Intuition, Bad Intuition—At the beginning of a relationship, your natural tendency might be a good guide. Once you really like the guy, your instinct might

betray you. You will and should have a desire for more physical intimacy.

Don't Panic

64. Here's the Panic Button. Don't Push It—Many women become so frightened of eternal singleness that they abandon their convictions and dive straight into relationship nightmares.
65. Never Buy a Swimsuit at a Hardware Store—Bars and clubs are poor places to find the love of your life.
66. Where Are the Princes Hiding?—Here are practical ideas for ways to meet quality men.
67. No Need to Get Married—You must adopt this attitude to live a happy life and not appear desperate to guys.
68. The Disease. The Cure—The number one struggle for women is poor self-esteem. A sure remedy is a relationship, but maybe not.
69. Loneliness and Sex—Gut wrenching loneliness with no hope in sight drives women to desperate actions.
70. Desperate Times, Desperate Actions—When they are desperate, women do regrettable things that may affect their marriage.
71. All Women Agree, But ... —No woman should be forced to do any act she does not want to do; yet, many women allow themselves to be controlled. Be sure you understand oral sex.

Rational Relationships

72. Here's a Quarter, Call Someone Who Cares—Seek the advice of close family or friends. They may not tell you what they think unless you ask.
73. Everybody Needs Counseling—Every couple will benefit by meeting with a counselor before you get married so you are less likely to need one after you are married.
74. Whatever—Beware of directionless, passive men.
75. Dating for the Worst Time in Your Life—Most of life is not a well-orchestrated date so consider how your guy will react to tough situations.

76. Online Toad Sorting—Explore the pros and cons of online matchmaking. It might be good.
77. To Find the Right Person, Be the Right Person—Men of character and integrity want a woman of character and integrity.
78. The Big Three: Love, Sex, and Money—The three biggest stumbling blocks.
79. So Sad to Belong to Someone Else when the Right One Comes Along—When you are in an exclusive relationship, you could miss the opportunity to connect with someone who is a better match.
80. You Will Marry Gutterslime. I Did—We all have serious flaws so don't expect your relationship, your marriage, your man, or yourself to be perfect. Trials and disappointments are guaranteed, no matter how wonderful he is.
81. Is That a Wart on Your Nose?—Girls can be as toxic as guys.
82. Lifestyles of the Rich and Famous and Confused—Celebrities are not reliable role models or sources of relationship wisdom. They are no smarter than you.
83. The Key to a Man's Heart—It's all about respect.
84. Every Divorce Begins with a Kiss—You may kiss the bride. Every divorced couple has a wedding album filled with smiling photos. You cannot judge a relationship by the optimistic and naive happy start. Is the marriage built on a firm foundation?
85. Spiritual Compatibility—If you have strong spiritual convictions, spiritual compatibility is a big deal.
86. An Impossible Journey?—Finding your prince can be extremely challenging. You might need spiritual support.

Cited Notes

[1] What's Love Got to Do with It?

1 Corinthians 13:4–6 The Living Bible

[2] Porn

Time Online Edition—"The Porn Factor" by Pamela Paul—January 19, 2004

www.familysafemedia.com/pornagraphy_statistics

www.blazinggrace.org

[3] STDs—Do the Math

Centers for Disease Control and Prevention (CDC). 2008 National STD Prevention Conference. Nationally Representative CDC Study Finds 1 in 4 Teenage Girls has a Sexually Transmitted Disease. March 11, 2008

[4] Hug the Wall

Associated Press Article—"Sex and Marriage" August 10, 2009 referring to National Longitudinal Study of Adolescent Health

[5] All Women Agree

Archives of Pediatrics & Adolescent Medicine, one of the JAMA/ Archives journals June 2010—Dr. Margaret Blythe, Indiana University School of Medicine

[6] All Women Agree

Washington Post—Laura Sessions Stepp, September 16, 2005

[7] All Women Agree

www.avert.org/oral-sex.htm

Acknowledgments

THE ANALOGIES IN this book are not all my own. I am not clever enough to think of all of them, but I can recognize a helpful illustration when I hear one. Since metaphors and examples are often repeated when they are particularly helpful, it can be difficult to know the originator of a cute concept. I can point out that the following metaphors did not originate with me. You may read more in these books to get the full effect.

Sex is like duct tape—J. Budziszewski, *Ask Me Anything: Provocative Answers for College Students*

Men are like waffles, women are like spaghetti—Bill and Pam Farrel, Book by the same title

Lifestyles of the rich and famous—Robin Leach

Men are microwaves, women are crockpots—Tommy Nelson, *The Book of Romance*

The love test, the red zone—Mike Long, *Everyone is NOT Doing It*

Stupid human tricks—David Letterman

To find the right person, you must be the right person—Emmerson Eggerich

"No decision you make in life will affect your future happiness or misery more than who you choose to marry."

—Unknown

I would like to thank the generous people who read my rough drafts and helped to steer me in the right direction: Brook Reid, John Keubler, J.D and Teresa Patton, Lynn Tobias, Linda Vaughn, Karen Montgomery, Marilla Showalter, Tim Frost, Dean and Janet Welty. Extra special thanks to Mike Thompson, Julie Barb, and Larry Leech for their thoughtful and detailed editing. None of the reviewers necessarily agree with everything I have written, but their insights helped sharpen concepts and spared me from embarrassing rough sections. Thank you Tristan Napotnik for the fun toad comics. Finally, thanks to my wife, Ruth, and my daughters for listening to my ideas more than they really wanted and reassuring me that the content is relevant.

Required Reading

Conversationally Speaking—Alan Garner

Recommended Reading

100 Questions to Ask Before You Get Engaged—Norman Wright
Boundaries in Dating—Drs. Cloud and Townsend
Sex and Dating—Mindy Meier
Too Close Too Soon: Avoiding the Heartache of Premature Intimacy—Jim A. Talley, Bobbie Reed
Love and Respect—Emmerson Eggerich
How to Win Friends and Influence People—Dale Carnegie
The Fine Art of Small Talk—Debra Fine
How to Talk to Anyone, Anywhere, Any time—Larry King
Intended for Pleasure—Ed Wheat (This book is for you to use when you are getting married)

Phone Helpline

800-A-FAMILY (800 232-6459)—Talk to friendly caring people. This is a free resource and referral service from Focus on the Family. I am not affiliated with Focus on the Family but I highly recommend them as a reliable resource.

Websites

www.prepinc.com PREP premarital counseling

www.smartmarriages.com Loaded with excellent articles about dating, relationships, and finding a mate.

www.family.org—Many excellent relationship resources in print and online and real live people counselors (Christian based)

www.slidingvsdeciding.blogspot.com—Research-based relationship advice, cohabitation emphasis

www.virginia.edu/marriageproject—Home of the National Marriage Project. Much research-based information about marriages, mate selection, sex, etc.

www.homeward.com—Practical relationship advice for all aspects of life (Christian based)

www.passionatecommitment.com—Honest, professional, tactful resource about marital sex

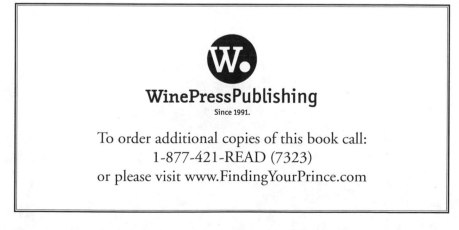